What people are saying about

Inner Brilliance, Outer Shine

Estelle is an excellent coach and trainer; her approach is practical and helpful and her passion for sharing everything she knows helps others to focus on what matters most in life. This must-read book provides hugely important skills for success in our personal and professional lives and shows us how to become a better version of ourselves.
Ali Brain, Joint Founder of Hannells, Award Winning Estate & Letting Agency

A thought-provoking read that highlight examples, our ability to recognise wha use that to 'shine'. By looking dee and then focusing on events, you are easy to follow toolkit designed to initially and and then take steps to action positive change. A -help book, that is logical to follow, practical and leaves the reader in control of 'destination joy'.
Andrew Bridge, Managing Partner of Fisher German LLP

Estelle's book is warm, wise and a wonderfully honest guide to living a full and balanced work-life. I would encourage you to let Estelle be your guide along the journey by sharing her hard-won lessons with real openness and courage. You will not be disappointed.
Professor Damian Hughes, International Speaker and bestselling Author

The MOT manual we should all have to read. Thank you, Estelle, you have changed my thinking and improved my world.
Dean Jackson, Owner and Founder of HUUB

If you are undecided about the effectiveness of coaching and coaching techniques, you absolutely need to read this book! Estelle gives us all some simple to use - yet hugely effective - tools to navigate our way through the ups and downs (or what she would call the still and choppy waters) of a life well-lived. I am the most cynical person I know but being introduced to Havening by Estelle and using this technique when the wheels are coming a bit loose has changed my life!

Sarah Parkinson, Equity Partner in a law firm

I feel like I just found the missing piece of the jigsaw down the back of the sofa. Having grappled with personal challenges around success and happiness for the best part of a decade, I have a profound sense that this book just changed my life for good! Refreshing. Inspiring. Honest. Witty. Challenging. Practical. Compelling reading from start to finish but even more so, compelling action focus.

Sarah Walker-Smith, CEO, Shakespeare Martineau LLP aka human being trying to do her best in life and business

Estelle Read's positivity and humour shine through in this brilliant book, and her openness about her recovery from workaholism really sets it apart. It shows how you can make profound changes to your feelings and behaviours, often very quickly. You *can* enjoy life and be successful too, and Estelle shows you how in her own accessible and enjoyable way.

Roz Watkins, Author of the DI Meg Dalton crime series

Inner Brilliance, Outer Shine

10 Antidotes to Imposter Syndrome, Workaholism and Stress

Inner Brilliance, Outer Shine

10 Antidotes to Imposter Syndrome, Workaholism and Stress

Estelle Read

BUSINESS
BOOKS

Winchester, UK
Washington, USA

JOHN HUNT PUBLISHING

First published by Business Books, 2021
Business Books is an imprint of John Hunt Publishing Ltd., No. 3 East St., Alresford,
Hampshire SO24 9EE, UK
office@jhpbooks.com
www.johnhuntpublishing.com
www.johnhuntpublishing.com/business-books

For distributor details and how to order please visit the 'Ordering' section on our website.

ISBN: 978 1 78904 803 2
978 1 78904 804 9 (ebook)
Library of Congress Control Number: 2021936359

A CIP catalogue record for this book is available from the British Library.

Design: Stuart Davies

UK: Printed and bound by CPI Group (UK) Ltd, Croydon, CR0 4YY
Printed in North America by CPI GPS partners

We operate a distinctive and ethical publishing philosophy in
all areas of our business, from our global network of authors to
production and worldwide distribution.

Contents

To the love of my life Michael Read. Thank you for the freedom and support to create and for always allowing me to be myself.
Also, to my little darling Daisy Read; you teach me to be a better human every day.

Foreword

So much is expected of us these days: to be great parents, innovative employees or successful business owners, to be fit and healthy, ready to face whatever the chaotic world throws at us. In this sea of change, we find ourselves drowning in demands, over-working, stressed and close to burn out. Even when we are 'successful' we can experience worry and fear about self-worth, which damages our ability to perform at our best and thrive. These competing bids for our mental resources cause old wounds to resurface, and past traumas to sabotage our success, as a result of limiting beliefs, behaviours and emotions. This book addresses those feelings which can make us believe we are unworthy of the success we have achieved.

Over the last three decades, I've been translating advances in neuroscience into new methods of healing. I am the creator (with my twin brother, Dr. Steven Ruden) of The Havening Techniques®, a psychosensory approach intended to eliminate the consequences arising from stressful or traumatic events. I continue to explore ways to use neuroscience to treat illness today. Havening Techniques can be used for more than emotional disturbances. They can aid wellness, assist in stress management, and boost performance.

In *Inner Brilliance, Outer Shine: 10 Antidotes to Imposter Syndrome, Workaholism and Stress* Estelle Read reveals how we can be brilliant in our own unique way. She has integrated the Havening Techniques, with many other solid coaching practices, and presents her sailing metaphor to help all business people regain their energy and general excitement about work-life, so they can achieve peak performance. She explains how we can offload unnecessary baggage and journey towards a work-life which is more joy-filled and rewarding.

To manage stress, reach peak performance and achieve goals, we recommend you use a professional coach that has been certified in The Havening Techniques. The Havening Techniques are powerful tools that can be used to treat the consequences of encoded traumatic or stressful memories. Depending on the nature of the encoded trauma it can be done with guidance by a certified Havening Techniques practitioner or by oneself. Estelle is a wonderful guide and coach, helping you traverse this challenging landscape.

Estelle has written an engaging guide on how to voyage towards your own version of Destination Joy, so that you are fully aligned towards your gifts and talents. She presents methods and tools for circumnavigating the rocks and handling the rough seas that we all face from time to time. She uncovers the strategies which act as antidotes to over-working so that you can attain more effortless success, be more personally effective and tap into your inner brilliance.

This is a must read for those who are ready to fully be themselves and shine naturally.

Ronald Ruden MD, Ph.D. Author of When the Past is Always Present

Acknowledgements

This book would not have been possible without The Havening Techniques® which have been pivotal in changing the lives of many. Thank you to Dr. Ronald Ruden the creator and Dr. Steven Ruden. Thanks also to the wonderful Feliciana Tello at Havening HQ; you are the jam in the sponge and bring everything together.

Thank you also to all the following: The Optimum Health Clinic, Ashley Meyer, Tony Burgess, Julie French, Irene Lambert, Michael Carroll, John Grinder and John Overdurf. You helped buff up *my* shine.

The wise Debbie Jenkins. Without your book coaching, I would have procrastinated another 10 years before this thing was written.

All my first readers and endorsees. This includes Michael Read, (my gorgeous, sage, rock of a husband for your unwavering belief, support and tolerance…not just during this project), Simone Jenkinson (my lovely cheerleading sister – you've no idea what a positive impact your comments made, so early on), Annette Jenkinson, (my strong, independent mum), John Jenkinson, (my innovative, fun-loving dad), Sarah Parkinson, (you gave me the kick up the rear I needed to get this project going again), Andrew Bridge, Alison Brain, Dean Jackson, Sarah Walker-Smith, Professor Damian Hughes, Roz Watkins, (for your insight into the publishing world and for encouraging me to 'get a proper publisher') and Mark Irving (my stoic cousin).

My 'crack team'. You helped me to hone the book title and its identity with your feedback. This includes Matthew Read and Louise Read, (my lovely stepson and daughter-in-law, for tolerating my digital ignorance and for your publishing advice), David Nelson, Maria Hawley, Dan Jarvis, Caitrina Oakes, Laura Iles, Fiona Ellis-Winkfield, Mike Reynolds, Liberty Stones, James

Willow, Alan Jones, James Bagley, Ruwangani Nagahwatte, Davina Ripton, Ben Brain, Liz Corcoran, Alison Darwent, Michelle Lewis, Petra Kalnai, Joanna McEwan, Harman Basra, Susan Clark, Beth Dickinson, Elizabeth Gale and Hannah Price.

Irena O'Brien for your neuroscience expertise and Trudy Bateman for your strengths research.

My Nana and Grandad. This is a bit of an odd one as they will never read this, but I must acknowledge their positive influence on me growing up. They both gave our family safety, stability, and a slice of the good life. My Nana would have loved to have told people about this book on the bus or at her history club, (she'd probably have carried a copy around in her handbag to whip out to strangers) and my grandad would have puffed his chest out with pride.

Finally, I would like to thank my fabulous clients. I love working with you; without your stories and inspirational change, there would be little stimulus to write. I feel privileged that I got to be a part of it. By the way, don't go trying to spot yourselves. My case study characters are a mixture of you all. x

Introduction

My client Charlotte drives from her executive home, in her executive car, to her executive coaching session. To the untrained eye, she is a success. She has made it in work and life and part-owns an award-winning business. She has a supportive husband and two children.

When she arrives, Charlotte stays in her car for 5 minutes so that she can hurriedly text her accountant. When she eventually comes in for her session, her neck and ears are flushed; outside clues as to how Charlotte is feeling inside.

She eventually sits in the 'coaching chair' and self-consciously adjusts her designer scarf to disguise her body's betrayal. The scarf is her crutch. However, her feelings escape again, this time her ankle begins to jerk anxiously. Charlotte announces that she must leave her phone on 24/7 for her clients.

Ten minutes into our coaching conversation, she takes a call. I don't know what the issue is, but my mirror neurons fire in empathy for her, enabling me to experience a waft of her stress. I feel tense and repeatedly adjust my physiology, so that I can be in a resourceful state for my coachee.

As she talks to her accountant, I start to wonder about the impact of Charlotte's emotional state on the people around her. She bravely shared in an earlier session, that in a recent 360 appraisal she'd been criticised for creating negative atmospheres. What was she like when she got home from work with her husband and kids? Was she leading a stressed state of mind in her team? How was she perceived by her clients and colleagues? But ultimately, I wondered what it must be like to be inside her body and mind.

Ever heard the saying, 'Takes one to know one'? I recognise the signs because I wore the t-shirt for 36 years. I made myself sick through overworking, over proving, overextending myself.

Recovery felt impossible. I felt convinced that I was going to spend a lifetime in bed or a wheelchair – because that was the worst-case scenario. I felt like a fraud – I was a coach for goodness sake! I'd been faking it and not made it. I'd failed. I was pushed to the edge. Reaching my tipping point forced me to face up to reality.

My client Charlotte had all the trappings of success but was miserable. Being stressed was her 'normal'. She'd got used to working herself into the ground because of imposter syndrome thoughts. Constantly switched on; it was alien for her to feel happy, calm, or joyful.

Charlotte never felt like she was enough and feared that one day her work-life would come tumbling down like a pack of cards and she would get found out. Being herself wasn't enough which created massive tension in her body. She pushed herself to the limits trying to belong and be accepted by others.

Her stress and anxiety were taking its toll on her body. She was experiencing panic attacks and a myriad of other undiagnosable symptoms. She was drinking heavily every night to soften her negative states and help her to relax. She hit rock bottom when she was admitted to hospital.

These physiological symptoms caused more anxiety and so the negative cycle continued.

Every moment was jam-packed either with work or home-life activities. Nobody in her family stopped. Each child participated in an impressive list of extracurricular activities, (all of which 'could' eventually turn into a career) and it was her job to ferry them about.

Charlotte was also a school governor and fully participated in all village social engagements, regardless of how dull they were. She wouldn't think twice about rustling up a Victoria sponge for the school fete at 11 pm. She really was a superwoman. Many people relied on her because she was a good egg and responsible. Being relied upon helped Charlotte's self-esteem, but gave her more to do.

The causes? She thought that people didn't like her. She didn't feel safe and secure enough to be herself. She'd learnt as a little girl that being herself, wasn't good enough. Her unconscious strategy to counter this was to do everything for everyone. She was looking for acknowledgement that she was a worthwhile person. She certainly wasn't shining. Charlotte looked as though she was heading towards a heart attack or nervous breakdown.

If our body is so filled with tension, pain, stress or anxiety; our mind never fully switching off because we have so much to do; is it any wonder that we're unable to fully access the joy of work and life? What is the point of continually striving and never arriving? What is the point of working so hard that we're too stressed and knackered to enjoy the fruits of our labour?

Good can come from adversity though and often there are connections in our childhood. We can grow from an experience. I learnt lots of new skills during my recovery. Having qualified as a coach, an NLP (Neuro Linguistic Programming) Practitioner, Master Practitioner and then eventually a Trainer of NLP, I'd been on a quest to sort myself out for a long while but still hadn't found *the thing* that fully hit the reset button. The technique which enabled me to be myself, without fear, judgement and fully embrace life without anxiety.

After being diagnosed with Myalgic Encephalomyelitis (M.E.), I learnt Integral Movement Therapy, Hypnotherapy, and EFT, (Emotional Freedom Technique) – this kick-started my recovery by beginning to remove excess baggage. But the thing that made the biggest difference was using the Havening Techniques®. Not only was it simple to use, but I could also treat myself! And it worked. And the change stuck. Suddenly, I could breeze into a situation without any conscious thought, which in the past had caused anxiety and lots of over-thinking about how awful it was going to be.

I also learnt and researched how to optimise my health and ultimately my performance at work. I took charge of the basics in life. How to sleep, eat and move effectively. Previously, I'd done these things on autopilot, not realising the impact it was having on my wellbeing.

Initially, I wanted to recover for my family. My daughter was 18 months old. *Then I realised I needed to do this for myself.*

Once I made that decision, my recovery began and co-incidentally I became a better wife, parent and coach. For the first time, I *really* started to love work and life. For the first time, I had moments where nothing was going on upstairs; no inner dialogue whirring away in the background, just silence. This silence enabled me to fully access the joy of tension-free work and life. It was such a novelty.

My energy grew; I went from being unable to climb the stairs to being able to achieve my ambition and get up a mountain and ski.

One of the best changes to my career came out of this adversity. I was able to work with clients so that they too experienced effortless change. No longer were they having to think through an alternative way of being at work, it simply occurred. Clients started talking about being 'Estelled' and began routinely reporting peace, tranquillity and even more success, but it was tension-free because they were being themselves.

This could just be a book about how you shine at work, but professional and personal lives are inextricably linked. One influences the other. If we have too much going on at home, our work suffers and vice versa. We are one person.

Initially, Charlotte had been very sceptical about the process and even doubted the changes she'd observed in herself. I had been noticing differences in her demeanour and language, (limiting beliefs had miraculously disappeared). She was no longer like a machine gun spattering out words in all directions. She was much more pleasant to be with and the scarf disappeared

– as did her blotchy neck. She'd stopped obsessing about her health and relationships. In fact, at the start of the session, she was silent. Then, she confirmed what I had suspected.

She said 'Things that I used to get embroiled in at work, no longer bother me. I don't seem to have as much to do. Even my friends patted me on the back for being honest about a subject that nobody else had been brave enough to raise. Ordinarily, I would have avoided saying anything, for fear of people not liking me.

I'm only drinking for pleasure at weekends, as opposed to using it to force relaxation. I've not had any panic attacks either. I feel at peace. I feel contented. I feel like myself.'

I don't profess to be Miss Perfect. I do slip up as you will see in the pages that follow, but the great thing is I have my blueprint for health, happiness, joy, self-esteem and how to move from stress to success. I no longer over-work or let feelings of imposter syndrome get in the way. I know how to get back on course. In this book, I will show you how to create your personal blueprint for these things too.

You will get rid of outdated programmes which create drag and prevent you from working and living most effectively. By applying the strategies that follow, your inner brilliance will shine through naturally.

It's time for an update. A reboot. A reset. A returning to the real you – just the way you were made. For you to be yourself. An alignment towards what makes you amazing. A deletion of the behaviours, beliefs and feelings that are dulling your shine. It is *your turn* to shine – now! It's *project me time*. You deserve and are entitled to lead your best work-life too, right?

Chapter 1

Antidote #1: Know Your Co-ordinates

If your boat is sinking, you really don't care in which direction it's pointed!
David Allen

Welcome to *project me time*! You're about to set sail on a voyage towards your version of joy-filled, tension-free, natural, work-life success. Each chapter will provide you with awareness and strategies that will help you to make this journey. I'm excited for you! Before you begin, you must establish where you are at now, because otherwise, how will you know where you want to travel to?

Also, in this chapter, I'm going to share with you the patterns of behaviour and thinking that prevent my clients from shining and attaining their desired change. These patterns are the things that in my coaching practice make my clients sink. Raising awareness of your patterns will help you to navigate your way around the rocks and steer clear of the sirens. You'll become the captain of your ship.

ACTION:

To get the most out of this book:

1. **Start by downloading my *Inner Brilliance, Outer Shine Workbook and Journal*,** which includes the exercises in this book and a place for you to note thoughts and actions: https://www.beee.company/resources
2. **Dedicate a time of day to read and complete the activities.** This is *project me time*!
3. **Join my Facebook group** of like-minded people and get

access to free content and live presentations https://www.beee.company/resources

4. **Take action!**

Writing your answers down will increase your chances of success, as opposed to passively reading and 'hoping' that the change will occur by itself. The workbook and journal will help you to capture your thoughts, feelings and learnings during your voyage and ensure you stay abreast of your co-ordinates. It will make Chapter 6 (where all the magic happens) so much easier when you start to get rid of the patterns of behaviour that are holding you back.

Change requires action! Go on. Do it now. Download the workbook: https://www.beee.company/resources

Groundhog Day: Screw up and Repeat

I was 18 months into running my own business and it was 11 am on a Saturday. I was stood in the doorway of our telephone box sized ensuite bathroom, as my husband got out of the shower. He was trapped and knew it. I was a sight for sore eyes. Still in my crumpled pyjamas, with lank hair and a face full of stress spots. He knows that look on my face. Glassy eyed and on the verge of tears. He said, 'I thought running your own business was meant to be fun! You look stressed again.' I'm drained, my body aches and the joy of work-life has vanished. These should have been warning signs, but I thought I was invincible. I took my health for granted. What I didn't realise was that I was slowly eating away at my resilience.

I'd been up since 4 am working on a culture change assignment for a client. The client was challenging and wanted the project delivering quickly. Being a pleaser with zero boundaries, I said yes to all his demands, which included facilitating sessions on consecutive days for several weeks. This meant any preparation had to be done in the evenings or at weekends – not to mention running my business and seeing other clients in between.

This scene was familiar because I'd ended up stressed in every job I'd ever had. I'd start off OK, but within 12 months the same old patterns would creep in: saying yes to anything and everything to prove my worth, which meant that I had to work long hours to accommodate the things I'd said yes to.

My boss in my last job asked me if I could write a course on Stress Management. When I began researching the subject, I realised I already had four books on the topic – one for each job. Every time stress built up, I would firstly blame it on the job and then go and buy a new book to find a magical cure.

Eventually, I realised the common denominator was me. I was a workaholic. My limiting beliefs, behaviours and feelings were weighing me down. My ship was at risk of sinking. I had too much baggage on board. I could no longer blame the organisation or boss for making me stressed – because I was now both those things.

Workaholism

Workaholics experience a compulsion to work hard, which results in excessive hours. The operative word being compulsion; it doesn't feel like a choice. Workaholics can experience guilt and anxiety when they are not working. Working helps to ease these feelings.

In a huge study which examined data on 16,426 working adults, they were able to identify connections between workaholism and mental illness. 'Workaholics scored higher on all the psychiatric symptoms than non-workaholics,' says researcher and Clinical Psychologist Specialist Cecilie Schou Andreassen, at the Department of Psychosocial Science, at the University of Bergen (UiB), and visiting scholar at the UCLA Semel Institute for Neuroscience and Human Behavior.

The study identified that workaholism frequently co-occurs with ADHD, OCD, anxiety, and depression.[1,2]

I used to wear my 'workaholic badge' as though it was something to be proud of. I loved telling people that I was sooooo busy. It made me feel indispensable. If you're wondering whether you are a workaholic, try answering the following questions.

ACTION:

Rate experiences occurring over the past year from 1 (never) to 5 (always):

- You think of how you can free up more time to work.
- You spend much more time working than initially intended.
- You work in order to reduce feelings of guilt, anxiety, helplessness or depression.
- You have been told by others to cut down on work without listening to them.
- You become stressed if you are prohibited from working.
- You deprioritise hobbies, leisure activities, and/or exercise because of your work.
- You work so much that it has negatively influenced your health.

If scored 4 or 5 points for at least four of the statements, the researchers suggest that it is time for an intervention! That intervention could be this book. You're in the right place.

ACTION:

Going forward, raise awareness of when you engage in any of the above habits. Review the questionnaire again, once you have completed this book.

Workaholics can feel inadequate, incompetent or simply not good enough. The workaholic can counter these feelings by proving they are enough and continually achieving. The problem with this is that they are trapped in a never-ending journey of striving but not arriving. They find it difficult to take in the seascape of their gifts, strengths and achievements.

I remember one of my very first coachees was an Equity Partner in a law firm. Not only was he an Equity Partner (this means you've made it), but he was the youngest Partner in the firm and yet he still wasn't enough. He was able to identify a friend in a law firm who'd made it as an Equity Partner much sooner than him.

You might be thinking that a workaholic is someone that simply loves what they do. There is a difference. A workaholic operates with tension and through compulsion. Often with my clients, there are connections in their childhood. I can remember being told in my school report, 'Estelle must try harder.' I was trying as hard as I flipping could! I didn't know how else to rectify the situation, so I tried harder by pressing down harder with my pencil. Anyone would think I was recording a Morse code distress message, scoring thick black smudged lines into my workbook.

The polar opposite of being a workaholic you might argue is a lazy layabout, which is not what I am proposing in this book. There is a sweet spot somewhere in the middle which enables us to become balanced and resilient workers. We can enter into that tension-free flow state, where we access the joy of work. Work is pleasurable and hobby-like, (most of the time). There is no inner obligatory voice telling you that you must, ought or should be working. Compulsion is replaced by choice. When it's time to stop working you can transition into home life and holidays more easily, without being distracted by thoughts about your job.

The tension I described earlier followed me through into adulthood, so much so that my neck almost disappeared into my shoulders and I eventually burnt out. In Chapter 6 you will learn about one of the antidotes to workaholism which will enable you to remove your compulsions to over-work using Havening.

Burnout

The World Health Organisation (WHO) has finally declared 'burnout' an official diagnosis. WHO describes it as:

'A syndrome conceptualized as resulting from chronic workplace stress that has not been successfully managed. It is characterized by three dimensions: 1) feelings of energy depletion or exhaustion; 2) increased mental distance from one's job, or feelings of negativism or cynicism related to one's job; and 3) reduced professional efficacy. Burn-out refers specifically to phenomena in the occupational context and should not be applied to describe experiences in other areas of life.'[3]

Stress

In an employee engagement study conducted by Kronos Incorporated and Future Workplace®, they discovered that 95% of HR leaders admit employee burnout is sabotaging workforce retention.[4] In another study, an estimated 60 to 90 per cent of doctor visits are to treat stress-related conditions.[5]

Most of my clients have some form of stress, which can be a catch-all phrase for any number of different states of mind. The words they use to associate with the umbrella term 'stress' have included:

- Angry or frustrated
- Anxious, nervous, apprehensive, worried, or panicked
- Suicidal, depressed, sad or unhappy
- Overwhelmed, exhausted or burnt out
- Insecure or lacking in confidence and self-esteem

When we are stressed, our sympathetic nervous system is switched on to enable our bodies to 'fight or flight'.[6] This was useful when we lived in caves and enabled us to avoid danger and survive. However, the 'dangers' we face today are much less life-threatening: it could be an email, a heated exchange with a colleague or the fact that your drive is blocked again by your neighbour.

Additionally, our work-lives are busier. The Telegraph said, 'Using the analogy of an 85 page newspaper, they found that in 1986 we received around 40 newspapers full of information every day but this had rocketed to 174 in 2007.'[7] This was based on a study conducted by Dr. Martin Hilbert and his team at the University of Southern California. Imagine how much we are processing today! It's no wonder people talk about feeling overwhelmed.

Whilst we are in fight or flight mode, our body is doing amazing things. We produce stress hormones including adrenaline, noradrenaline and cortisol. Our heart rate increases, pupils dilate, muscles tighten and we breathe more quickly. This enables us to deal with any 'threats' we are presented with. However, the challenge arises when we don't learn to switch this system off by being constantly busy and not managing our stress; it causes health issues. This can be anything from backache, headaches, blood pressure, irritable bowel syndrome, heartburn...the list goes on. A 2015 study revealed that workplace stress kills 120,000 people a year.[8]

Not only does stress impact on our health, but it also changes our behaviour too. We might be short with our work colleagues, clients, family and friends or bury our feelings in shopping, alcohol, food, sex, gambling or work. Everyone is unique in terms of what triggers their stress, and the strategies they use to deal with it.

For our body to return to a balanced state known as 'homeostasis' following stress, we need to trigger the relaxation response, which is run by our parasympathetic nervous system. The body can only heal itself when this system is triggered, hence why we are susceptible to more illness when we are stressed. Talk about kick a person when they are down! We'll be looking at how to be more relaxed in Chapter 10.

The first step in any change is to raise awareness of what's going on. You are going to use this awareness to put you back in charge of the results you are getting. Therefore, don't do what I did and ignore the signals from your body; they serve a purpose:

- **Trust your body**, don't doubt.
- **Pay attention**, try to understand, don't suppress.
- **Take corrective action**, don't power on through.

ACTION:

The great news is that the body has an amazing ability to heal and recover. In Chapter 10 we'll look at how you can take care of your body but for now, begin tuning in:

- On a scale of 1 – 10, (10 being extremely) how:
  - Stressed do you feel?
  - Exhausted do you feel?
  - Disengaged, i.e. detached or unmotivated, do you feel with your job?
- Do you have any physical signs of stress, e.g. acne, headaches, migraines, chronic pain, a tendency to pick up bugs, insomnia, changes in libido or appetite, rapid heartbeat, IBS, etc?

Review the above assessment once you have finished this book to see what's changed.

An Inside Job

If we point the finger of blame as to the cause of our current situation, we give our power away, because the source of our problem is outside us. We are relying on the situation clearing up with the passage of time, (which of course it can do), someone rescuing or solving the issue for us, or we keep running. We keep changing external stuff in the hope that our internal stuff will get better.

When I was employed as the Head of Human Resources at a law firm, each time I felt insecure or worried about something, I would pop down to the Managing Partner's office for a chat. I was reliant on his encouraging words (external stuff) to make me feel better.

My boss was a kind man and very astute at making character assessments. As someone who practised childcare law, he was used to interpreting what wasn't being said. One day, as I sat twisting like a 5-year-old on my office chair, he said, 'You've come for a pep talk, haven't you?' I felt so embarrassed. I'd been found out.

Craving Reassurance

He was holding the mirror up. At that moment I realised that my self-esteem was reliant on what other people thought of me. I would go on and on, trying to prove that I was good enough, an OK person and that people valued my contribution. I was trapped in a cycle of justifying my existence. This was a flawed plan. I had resigned from my position and was about to set up my own company, Beee. I wouldn't have anyone to tell me I was doing OK, once I started working on my own.

If the only way we can maintain our self-esteem and stay afloat is by relying on the positive reassuring buoyancy aids that other people throw us, what happens when there's nobody around, or they forget? We can feel resentful that people aren't more forthcoming. We become vulnerable when the waters get choppy and we're exhausted. We're also not in charge of when people throw us those acknowledgements. If we are building competency in a new skill, feedback is important. However, if we're in the habit of craving reassurance having already built competence, that probably needs looking at. Just as an addict needs their drugs to feel OK, we mistakenly get trapped in a cycle of needing praise to feel OK.

Notice how I don't say, awesome, amazingly talented being. The clients that fit into the group of people I am writing this book for, (I include my old self here too), wouldn't dream of thinking that way. The imposter within is always undermining, doubting and keeping any positive thoughts about themselves at bay. They get used to minimising themselves. Shrinking the space that they occupy.

Shrinking Your Space

Have you ever sat in one of those swanky car showrooms? I love to people watch. I'm half working, half listening in to some of the conversations, and take time to notice those that shrink and take over space.

For example, some people talk loudly and importantly on their mobile phones, quite happy to disturb the peace of others, impolitely continuing their conversation whilst the service technician waits patiently. You could argue they are owning their space. I would argue that they are invading space…disrespectfully taking the time and energy of others. They come from a position of superiority and arrogance. No feelings of imposter syndrome going on here. Flash Harry/Henrietta acting like they own the place, never mind your spot! These are the characters we need to be on alert for: time and space stealers. We'll look at how we manage our time and people boundaries in Chapter 7.

Then there are those at the other end of the spectrum who look unsure. Nervously darting their eyes around the showroom wondering what the protocol is for getting a fancy coffee. Then apologising for disturbing the barista and asking them to do their job. Shrinking their body and voice; moving in an uncomfortable, self-conscious way. Unable to acknowledge that they are entitled to be there too. Not recognising that their hard-earned cash is as worthy as anyone else's sat in that waiting area. They feel as though they don't belong. They feel like an imposter. More about this in a moment.

ACTION:

- Where, when and with whom do you feel like an imposter?
- Under what circumstances do you minimise your needs, feelings, views or opinions?
- How do you minimise yourself?
- What causes you to minimise yourself?
- Who or what do you rely on, (external to you), to bolster your self-esteem?

Imposter Syndrome

I once worked with a client called Mark who was on the board of a PLC. Again, pretty successful, ay? However, when I met him it was as though he was apologising for his existence; he said sorry half a dozen times in the space of 90 seconds.

As I began exploring how his behaviours played out at work, he said he felt 'invisible.' I am intrigued by metaphors that people use to describe themselves and how they embody what they believe through their actions and behaviour.

Mark wanted to have more presence in the boardroom. I asked him to describe the scene during meetings with the board. He said that he would typically turn up last minute in a fluster, sit in the least obvious position around the table and would then physically move his chair back, away from the group, so that he was invisible. He would also make his physiology as small as possible and take on the role of a submissive note taker.

I fed back my observations and asked him how long he had been justifying his existence and feeling 'invisible' and he said, 'Since I was a little boy. I was told that I should sit on the reserve bench and wasn't good enough to play.'

Mark had imposter syndrome going on. Have you ever looked around and wondered, *What am I doing here? Do I deserve this? Should I be at this, boardroom table, fancy social event, company etc? Surely, someone is going to tap me on the shoulder and tell me that there's been a mistake; that I don't belong.*

My first career experience of imposter syndrome was when I was 20. The business was running an organisational change initiative to encourage employees to cut costs. I was working for a company that made cellulose acetate for photographic film and the MD (my now husband), told us about the emergence of digital photography, (which I thought sounded like science fiction) and how it was going to be tough for our industry to survive – hence the initiative.

There were a limited number of places on the programme and much to my surprise I was selected, as someone had dropped out and I was the understudy. I had managed to brush this fact aside, when I overheard a colleague in the loos saying, 'What's that piddly Estelle doing on the course? She's the most junior person in the organisation! What contribution can she make?'

People with imposter syndrome attribute their success and achievements down to luck, or others mistakenly believing they are better than they are. The term was first coined by Dr. Pauline R. Clance and Dr. Suzanne A. Imes in their 1978 article and it was thought initially that it used to impact high achieving women.[9] Since then it has been identified that it affects both men and women equally.

Imposter syndrome is something I see often in my office. I sit astonished as I listen to my clients, who are usually already very successful, undervalue themselves. It's almost as though they have a form of work dysmorphia. Take Leo for example, who was a Partner in one of the largest law firms in the UK. He earnt as much as I made in a year, in his bonus. And yet, he still hadn't made it. He still wasn't a success. In his head, he still wasn't valued by the firm he part-owned! He still wasn't enough.

Not Good Enough

The underlying limiting belief with many of my clients is: I'm not good enough.

Trudy Bateman, Head of Strengths Profile at Cappfinity says,

'According to the research by Cappfinity in 2019 using 60,000 Strengths Profiles, Self-belief was one of the most common weaknesses of the 60 strengths.' I'll be telling you more about this strengths profile in Chapter 4.

In my eyes, Leo was an amazingly courageous, talented, passionate and brilliant individual. However, he too was exhausted, had lost his work mojo and massively doubted his contributions and their worth. He wasn't shining.

ACTION:
- When, where and with whom are you enough?
- When, where and with whom, aren't you enough?
- How will you know when you are enough? What evidence will there be?
- What will cause you to stop the pursuit of *enoughness*?

My aspiration for all my clients is for them to *really* see themselves for what they are. All their wonderfulness. To be able to accept their gifts, talents and achievements. For them to accept where they do a great job.

And, when things don't go well, to be able to comfortably accept this too, without brandishing themselves a failure or damaging their self-esteem. Nobody is perfect. We all have foibles.

I believe we *all* have the potential to be brilliant in our own way. We can't all have the same talents and abilities – which is great news! We need to celebrate our uniqueness and stop denying our greatness. Embrace it. Own it.

Getting Stuck in Denial
One of the thinking traps, which prevents change in my clients is denial. Denial of their treasure trove of talents and abilities. Denial that something needs to change. When I first got diagnosed with ME it was tough. I felt scared. I was aware that

some patients spent years in bed and had to use a wheelchair. For some, their body had given up completely and they died. There were days when I could have happily stayed in bed, probably for weeks. I could barely walk across the road. I was unable to lift my daughter out of her car seat. I didn't have the strength to make the beds. I had to sit on the floor whilst I emptied my laundry bin. Little things I'd totally taken for granted. I had to stop in lay-bys and car parks to sleep. This was out of character as a person that is typically known for being high energy, excitable and a busy knickers.

I paid for a ME recovery programme and they estimated that it would take me 18 months to get better. I was determined to get well, quicker; I thought I could buck the trend – always the achiever, even during illness! I can remember saying to my husband, 'It's not going to take me 18 months to recover. Anyway, I don't have time to be ill!' So, I booked myself into a health spa for three days and thought, *that'll do it*. I'm sat here laughing as I type this. I was both naive and arrogant.

I'd checked into the spa and was sat in what can only be described as a chintzy, Barbie Doll hotel bedroom. I was waiting to speak to my nutritionist. As part of my treatment, I'd had my adrenal glands tested and she was calling to give me the results.

The phone began vibrating on the plastic bedside cabinet. It was my nutritionist. As she spoke, I was willing her to tell me it was all in my head, the diagnosis had been a big mistake and there was nothing wrong with me. It was one of those conversations that seemed to be playing out in slow motion, as she confirmed that my adrenals were about as worn out as they could have been. She said 'for them to be in this state, you must have stressed for a very long time.'

I couldn't connect to what the nutritionist was saying. I didn't feel stressed. I couldn't think of any big events that could have caused my stress. This was because I was perpetually stressed – that was my 'normal'. I had no measure of not being that way. At that moment, I reached my tipping point.

I felt like a failure, a fraud and was ashamed. I was a Coach and Personal Effectiveness Trainer for goodness sake. And yet here I was completely ineffective and stressed. Not exactly a shining example!

I realised that I'd been faking it but never making it. A previous boss once said I had a 'plastic smile'. Looking back, she was right. Put a smile on, get your head down, don't complain and avoid any uncomfortable feelings by keeping busy.

Over-working was a way of keeping my anxiety at bay. Being busy was a way of adding to my self-worth. I was justifying my existence by being useful to people. However, I was so busy and stressed that I damaged myself and left my body in a defenceless state, which meant that after an infection and 15 varieties of antibiotic, I contracted ME.

Following the nutritionist's diagnosis, she recommended all sorts of changes to my diet. I had to give up caffeine, dairy, certain grains, sugar, alcohol, anything processed – all the good stuff. I thanked her for her advice and pushed everything she said to one side. I thought she was exaggerating and that her recommendations were extreme and for other people. I was still questioning whether I was ill. I was stuck in denial.

My normal way of being was under threat. The people at the clinic kept talking about a 'new me' once I'd completed the M.E. recovery programme. I didn't want a new me; I wanted to be able to go back to the old me. You know, the one that rushed around like a blue-arsed fly, achieving lots to prove I was good enough. The one that didn't know how to really enjoy work-life because I was constantly moving the goalposts of what good enough meant. The one that suppressed any feelings of inadequacy by working harder and full of tension. Sounds so attractive, doesn't it? I didn't know all of that until I moved beyond denial. If we deny what's going on for us, we don't need to take alternative action.

Elizabeth Kubler-Ross, a Doctor in Switzerland studied dying people and discovered that when we experience loss, we go through a cycle of emotional states.[10] In the ensuing years, it was found that we can experience these emotional states in a variety of situations when we receive bad news or face difficult change. This could be anything ranging from hearing negative feedback from your boss to learning about the loss of a loved one.

I have seen several iterations of the Kubler-Ross Cycle. I find this one useful in business:

- Stage 1: Shock, denial and rejection of facts.
- Stage 2: Anger, defensiveness and pointing the finger of blame.
- Stage 3: Rationalisation. The realisation of the inevitable, which leads to negative feelings.
- Stage 4: Acceptance. Ready to plan and explore solutions.
- Stage 5: Growth. Changes have been implemented and integrated.

When I work with my corporate clients, I ask the coachee's sponsor to complete a form which gets them to explain what the current issues are and where they would like the coachee to move to. Not only is the coachee potentially receiving bad news but they are faced with change – the desired outcome from the sponsor's perspective.

I then get the sponsor to share this information with the client before they come to their coaching session. This is because of the Kubler-Ross Cycle. I want them to have had time to digest the feedback so that they are moving towards 'Acceptance' above.

With most of my clients, this works like a treat. However, Elizabeth ended up losing her position because she got stuck in denial. Accepting the feedback given by her boss would have meant that she was wrong, and she *always needed to be right*. That was part of the reason she had been sent for coaching. Her over-bearing style was having an impact on her team, to the extent where they'd given up trying to solve problems or use their initiative. She operated a 'my way or the highway' style of leadership. Additionally, they would get screeched at if they made mistakes.

When she arrived for her session there were no social niceties. She stood on my doorstep with flared nostrils, drumming her perfectly manicured nails against my porch. She said, 'This is going to be a complete waste of time!' and marched past me up to my office.

We started the session by re-visiting the sponsor goals and feedback. She was able to provide counter-arguments for every point made by her boss.

I tried a different tack. I could support what had been said by the sponsor, because I'd seen how Elizabeth operated in the business and on my doorstep. I gave my feedback too, in the hope that she would move on from denial. I fed back behaviours I had seen and heard with my own eyes and ears – *no wriggling out of this!* To my surprise, she continued to stay stuck in denial.

I showed Elizabeth the Kubler-Ross Cycle and explained how we can get stuck in denial when we receive feedback but reassured her that it was completely normal. She said the model was 'A load of old poppycock.'

In a last ditched attempt, I explained that I'd observed her denying feedback in the session. Her response, 'No I don't.'

We worked for a few sessions, but in the end, I realised the business was wasting their money. She'd got stuck in denial and blamed everyone else. Some people get stuck for years. She wasn't prepared to come off autopilot and steer her ship. Consequently, several months later, she ended up at Destination Grim. She was side-lined. Ring-fenced away from the rest of the team to limit the damage. Her fear of failure became a self-fulfilling prophecy.

ACTION:

So, what are your coordinates?

- Where are you right now in work-life?
- Score your current level of happiness out of 10 (10 = couldn't be better) for:
  - Work
  - Personal life
- Where are you stuck?
- What are you denying needs to change?

Summary of Key Points:

- Tune into your workaholic habits. Use the quiz as a reminder. How could you reduce your score?
- Pay attention and trust the signals from your body. How does your body feel right now? How do you generally feel physically and mentally? What changes could you make?
- Who or what do you blame for your current situation? What is within your power and control to change?
- Be aware of when you are shrinking the space in which you occupy. This could be a clue imposter syndrome is at play. Then expand to and own your space. Physically broaden out your body.
- Reflect on when is enough, enough? When will you be good enough? What evidence will you have?
- How can you begin to acknowledge your gifts, talents and achievements?
- Don't get stuck in denial. What are you denying needs to change right now, that is within your control? Recognise when change is necessary. You can do it. Science says so!

Chapter 2

Antidote #2: Captain Your Ship

You must take personal responsibility. You cannot change the circumstances, the seasons, or the wind, but you can change yourself. That is something you have charge of.
Jim Rohn

We have a motorboat which is moored in the Lake District. She is affectionately known as our caravan on water. My husband tends to be the captain (aka Evel Knievel – he likes speed). I am the health and safety officer. When Evel Knievel gets carried away and breaks the 10 nautical miles an hour speed limit, I take the helm. In this chapter, we are going to look at how you too can take the wheel and be the captain of your ship, so that you prevent it from sinking or crashing on the rocks.

When it's the three of us on board our boat it is very stable and easy to drive. However, the health and safety officer inside me goes into overdrive when we have extra bodies on board; it can feel like it's going to keel over. There was an incident on a supposedly sedate tour of the Lake. I turned around to find my 91-year-old Nana flailing about like a rag doll and at risk of bouncing off the back. I took the helm.

The more people and baggage on board the more unstable the boat becomes and the greater the drag. It is an inefficient way of cruising. The boat has a weight limit in the instruction manual to prevent it from sinking. In this chapter, we are going to look at how to best operate *your ship*.

Your Ship

We too are at risk of sinking if we are overloaded with work, caused by limiting beliefs, behaviours and emotions. Let me introduce you to your Ship which contains many things:

- **Your Autopilot** is your unconscious mind. Everything that takes place here is automatic and without conscious awareness or thought.
- **Your Captain** is your conscious mind and is responsible for taking charge of your results, making decisions, steering your Ship towards your desired outcome and away from your workaholic habits. The Captain *takes positive action*.
- **Your Inner Captain** is the voice inside your head and includes the words you use and tonality. Your Inner Captain will learn to squash imposter syndrome thoughts.
- **Your Bridge** is the command centre of your Ship, which receives information from both internal (bodily sensations, thoughts and feelings) and external sources (what you see, hear, smell, taste and touch). Being able to tune into this information when you need to, enables the Captain to make well-informed decisions. The Bridge represents your self-awareness.
- **The Crow's Nest** symbolises your ability to become the objective observer; more mindful as opposed to getting lost or overwhelmed by an experience. This is important as you begin to make connections with memories and your present-day behaviour, beliefs and emotions.
- **Your Treasure Trove** represents your gifts, talents, strengths and achievements. You are going to learn to accept and embrace these.
- **Your Baggage** includes the past experiences that are weighing you down, creating drag on your Ship and still influencing you today. Relax and be easy; we all have baggage.

The tools available to help you navigate through this book include:

- *The Inner Brilliance, Outer Shine Journal.* This is used for writing down your observations, thoughts, feelings, learnings, memories and actions, to resolve any issues identified. You can download this here: https://www.beee.company/resources
- *The Inner Brilliance, Outer Shine Workbook* which includes the activities and questions from this book. You can download this here https://www.beee.company/resources

I'm going to introduce you formally to all the above metaphors throughout the book.

Your Ship is the vessel which carries you to your destination. Most human beings do this on Autopilot, and if they're lucky, things work out for the best. For others, they can end up at Destination Grim. Or you can take charge of your desired outcomes in work-life and consciously steer your Ship towards Destination Joy.

In Chapter 6 you will begin offloading any excess Baggage which is weighing you down and steering you in the wrong direction. Excess Baggage creates drag on your Ship and for some, makes them sink. This extra and outdated Baggage (more about this in Chapter 3), makes the journey slower, less enjoyable and takes more fuel and effort. Hence why when this Baggage is removed, success feels more effortless and natural.

Owner-ship of Your Treasure Trove

When a ship is first registered, its country of origin is documented. Its nationality allows a ship to travel internationally, as it is proof of ownership.

Our Ship contains our Treasure Trove of gifts, talents and

achievements. If we don't own-our-Ship, and all it has to offer, how do we know where we can travel to? I hear so many clients rejecting and minimising their talents, abilities, strengths, achievements and compliments. They undervalue themselves because of their imposter syndrome thoughts. They give off the wrong vibes. All that self-doubt causes doubt in others. It's the equivalent of walking through Border Force under the 'Nothing to Declare Sign', looking guilty as hell because you're worried you might get found out or stopped, but actually, genuinely have nothing to declare! I hear my clients claiming responsibility and assigning blame to themselves, for problems that aren't theirs. Then some seem to sail through going under the radar without a second thought.

When we don't declare ownership of our gifts, talents and achievements (and I don't mean in a foghorn way; to ourselves) it damages our self-esteem. When our self-esteem is damaged, we give off the wrong vibes. I say to my clients it's the equivalent of holding a white surrender flag above our head which says 'It's OK to take advantage of me.' Because of our work hard ethic, we gain the reputation of being a good egg who will do anything for anyone, is reliable and always delivers on a promise. Our needs are forgotten because we are busy putting everyone else's needs first. In fact, we've spent that much time thinking about what everyone else wants, we don't know what our needs are. You're going to home in on your needs in Chapters 4 and 5. For now, what gifts, talents and achievements do you need to take *owner-ship* of?

ACTION:

- What have you achieved that you are proud of?
- What are your gifts and talents?
- How can you begin to acknowledge your gifts, talents and achievements?

At the end of each day, try writing down all the things you did well in *The Inner Brilliance, Outer Shine Journal* – capture your observations, thoughts, feelings, learnings and actions to resolve any issues identified. More about this in Chapter 8.

Coming off Autopilot

To start to own and take charge of our Ship, we need to come off Autopilot, which is run by our unconscious mind. Bruce Lipton PhD, former medical school professor, research scientist and author of The Biology of Belief proposes that we operate from our Autopilot 95% of the time.[11] However, this can be as much as 99% if the person has low self-awareness, which I will come onto shortly. 'An enormous portion of cognitive activity is non-conscious, figuratively speaking, it could be 99 per cent; we probably will never know precisely how much is outside awareness,' says Dr. Emmanuel Donchin, director of the Laboratory for Cognitive Psychophysiology at the University of Illinois.

Our Autopilot is the thing that enables us to communicate, make decisions, carry out tasks, act and emote without thinking. It received a good chunk of our behaviour, belief and emotion programming by the age of seven, through our experience and the people around us. These programmes enable us to act without consciously thinking. For example, automatically agreeing to do anything that is asked of us with a smile on our face. Piling up our to-dos. Extending productivity hours without a second thought about the personal consequences. So, what if we miss that planned session at the gym, or catching up on our favourite TV programme, or having time to make a home-cooked meal, or putting the kids to bed or being able to see a friend.

Before long, the stuff we do to rest and recharge, to re-invigorate, to rejoice in this amazing thing we call life, diminishes. We're on that constant loop of work and sleep – that's if you're lucky enough to not be waking up in the night thinking about all the things you haven't done!

When I run my stress management courses and I ask the audience, 'When was the last time you had fun?', they tend to look at each other in confusion or say 'Fun is for children.' They even ask me to clarify what I mean. I will say things like, 'You know, the last thing that made you go weeeeeee in your head, (or even better out aloud), like for example, flying down your first blue-run or cantering on a horse.'

We sacrifice time for ourselves for time for work. Breaking this habit requires us to consciously raise awareness of any limiting beliefs, behaviours and feelings. This awareness helps us to take back the helm and be in charge of the outcomes we're getting. Otherwise, we are ships without a captain, wondering how we ended up at a Destination Grim. We can then change our automatic programmes either through conscious repetition until we develop a new habit, which is then handed over to your Autopilot, or we cheat and use Havening!

The neuroscience explaining the detailed functioning of the brain is extremely complex and beyond the scope of this book. Here I use a simplified model to explain the functions of the unconscious mind, which has connections with the work of John Grinder and Richard Bandler, the co-creators of NLP (Neuro Linguistic Programming), a communication and personal development model.

The Unconscious Mind

Your unconscious mind can do amazing things outside of your conscious awareness

- **Simultaneous processing.** According to Bruce Lipton, we are unconsciously processing 40 million bits of data per second.[12] A piece of data could be your left big toe, pressing against your footwear, (which you may now have become consciously aware of). All this information comes in through your senses and these processes inform our 'intuition'. For example, you may have interviewed someone and instinctively knew that the person wasn't right for the role or organisation, but then struggled to immediately articulate why. That is until the information bubbled up into your conscious mind often when you least expect it, like in the shower.

• **Non-verbal communication.** The unconscious mind conveys what you think through your body language, such as looking at your watch when you are wondering how long a meeting will go on for. Some people have had training to mask their body language; to cover up what they are really thinking and feeling. However, this is when we can start to look incongruent with the message we are trying to communicate and is why politicians can come across as being insincere and unbelievable. I'll be talking about when it is beneficial to change your body language in Chapter 7.

• **Store our memories and past experience which can inform or damage our future.** For example, those childhood events which created our values and beliefs. We'll take a deeper dive into these in Chapter 4. Our brain has an amazing ability to make connections with similar experiences so that we have a neural network of events which relate to the same belief, e.g. I'm not good enough. We'll begin to 'trim' any unhelpful neural pathways in Chapter 6.

• **Produce automatic emotions, actions, skills, behaviours and habits. Anything we become competent at and can do without thinking.** If you've been driving for a while, I bet you drive to work unconsciously. Did you say to yourself: mirror, signal, manoeuvre or did you arrive at your destination without thinking? That's your Autopilot. Once we become unconsciously competent at a task, activity, behaviour or way of responding emotionally to a situation, our unconscious mind takes care of it. This is where we can get into bad habits because our unconscious will take the path of least resistance, i.e. where there is a well-established way of being; an entrenched set of neural pathways, it is easier for the unconscious mind to take that route. This is why behaviour change takes repetition or using something like Havening to 'cheat', so that you diminish the unhelpful neural pathways, enabling new ones to flourish.

- **Run our autonomic system** which is responsible for the control of our bodily functions not consciously directed, such as breathing, pumping our heart and digestive processes. It's the system that allows our fight or flight system to slam on our breaks when a pheasant decides it would be a good time to cross the road. Imagine how exhausting it would be if we had to control all these things consciously!

ACTION:

To come off Autopilot start to tune into your language as it will be an indication of what you really think or believe about yourself at a deeper level. For example, if you catch yourself saying, 'I won't bore you with...', this could mean that you think you are boring or uninteresting. Another example would be 'It doesn't matter...' this could mean that you think you don't matter.

- What things do you automatically say, which may be a clue as to what you really think or believe about yourself?
- Consider whether there are connections with imposter syndrome.
- Also, use coming off Autopilot to continue to raise awareness of any workaholic habits.

This is all useful information for when you start to clear up limiting beliefs, behaviours and emotions in Chapter 6.

Your Captain is Calling

For the purposes of this book, your conscious mind is represented by your Captain. The role of your Captain is to:

- Navigate *more intentionally* away from Destination Grim towards Destination Joy. You will define what this is for you in Chapter 5.
- Take charge and make your desired change happen. Don't be passive in this process. *You have to take action*. To begin with, that means completing the activities in this book. You can download *The Inner Brilliance, Outer Shine Workbook* and *The Inner Brilliance, Outer Shine Journal* here: https://www.beee.company/resources

Some scientists believe we are between 1% – 5% consciously in charge of our actions…and 5% is for the more self-aware. Most operate at 1% consciousness. No wonder we end up marooned at Destination Grim. We don't do it on purpose. It's simply a lack of either not knowing we can take charge or we play victim or persecutor. More later about these patterns which keep us stuck and unable to lead the work-life we desire.

If we are only 1% consciously in charge of our actions, imagine what we could do if we increased this to 5%. This is great news! It allows you to do and be something different. To get better results. To change your workaholic habits. To reduce your stress. To diminish your imposter syndrome thoughts. To get comfortable in your own skin. To enjoy work and life more.

Let's get to know your Captain so that you know what it is capable of.

The Conscious Mind

Your conscious mind is:

- Logical and uses common sense
- Linear and thinks in straight lines
- Able to process around 40 bits of information per second[13]
- Rational, analytical and questioning
- Deliberate, decides and directs
- Able to *organise* and *give direction* to the unconscious mind

Here lies another opportunity. We need to ensure that your Captain programmes your Autopilot effectively. This is why in Chapter 5 you will identify Destination Joy through a series of goals and a vision. It is also why you will get to grips with your Inner Captain in Chapter 8, to ensure the words you use in your head, give the right direction to your Autopilot. If your programming is naff, your output is at risk of being naff too.

Additionally, in Chapter 6 you will be able to suppress the neural pathways connected to limiting beliefs, behaviours or emotions using Havening. This will change your unconscious programming and support you to develop new habits and behaviours.

To give positive direction to your Captain and stretch your conscious control to 5%, you are going to need great self-awareness. I'll refer to your awareness as the Bridge and it will work in conjunction with your Captain.

Your Bridge

The Captain can often be found on the Bridge when difficult manoeuvres are required. The Bridge is the command centre of your Ship and represents your self-awareness. Your Bridge receives information from many sources both *internally* (bodily sensations, thoughts, and feelings) and *externally* (what you see, hear, taste, smell and touch).

Being aware of this information enables the Captain to make well-informed decisions, for example, when you have something difficult to say, (this will become important when you get to Chapter 7).

The best communicators are those with high emotional intelligence and are positioned on their Bridge. They are tuned into how their message is being heard, by observing the other person's body language, voice tone and words (external information received by the Bridge).

This information prompts the Inner Captain to reflect and consider, *is this conversation going well, or not so well? What should I do next to get this conversation back on track?* (internal information received by the Bridge).

The Captain then makes a decision based on the information received from the Bridge and takes action, e.g. smiles and says, 'Hey, I've miscommunicated what I wanted to say. Let me put this another way.'

From the Bridge, you will be able to detect when you are mindlessly going through an experience. For example, being on a beautiful walk, but not noticing the beauty because you are busy thinking about something that happened at work.

You can use your Bridge to tap into how your body is feeling and performing, as opposed to ignoring that ache in your shoulder. This is communication from your Ship; it's telling you to stop doing something!

Your Bridge can be used to tap into the beliefs, behaviours and emotions at play when you have been triggered or something isn't working for you. For example, if you believe you are *boring* which results in you not speaking up in a meeting (this is the behaviour) and then feeling frustrated afterwards, you would use your Bridge to raise awareness of this. Your Captain would then have some decisions to make. Do you ignore the seven iceberg warnings like the captain of the Titanic[14] and carry on sailing regardless, or divert and do something different?

Sometimes we become blind to what's really going on for us. We suppress and delete the truth. I'm suggesting that where work and life could be better, you look at things with a fresh pair of eyes. The idea of your Bridge is that having received the information, your Captain can:

- Assess whether something is working or not and take corrective action where necessary.
- Programme your Autopilot, so that you end up at Destination Joy, as opposed to Destination Grim.

One of the decisions your Captain may make based on information from your Bridge is when to use the Crow's Nest, so that you lessen the impact of an emotional experience.

The Crow's Nest

In Daniel Goleman's book *Emotional Intelligence*, he talks about the importance of self-observation, 'At a minimum, it manifests itself simply as a slight stepping-back from experience, a parallel stream of consciousness that is "meta": hovering above or beside the main flow, aware of what is happening rather than being immersed and lost in it.'[15]

I love Daniel's description. This is the type of observation I'd like you to use as you begin to raise your awareness of limiting beliefs, behaviours and feelings and where they come from. This is so that you lessen the impact of old feelings until you are ready to deal with them in Chapter 6.

For example, sometimes clients can have an abreaction when they think deeply about something from their past, resulting in them getting upset. To reassure you, crying is perfectly fine in my coaching practice, especially when someone has been repressing and hanging onto old stuff for so long. Sometimes acknowledging and releasing the emotion in a safe place is all a person needs, to move on.

However, if you allow yourself to become fully absorbed back into negative memories associated with a limiting belief, behaviour or emotion and don't deal with it there and then, it could make you feel bad. Only allow yourself to become immersed if you are using a technique to clear the memory and triggers such as Havening or EFT, which we will come onto in Chapters 6 and 9. For traumatic memories, I would always recommend seeking out a qualified Havening or EFT Practitioner.

To adopt the Crow's Nest position, simply imagine you are floating above an experience or memory (or to the side if you are afraid of heights). *Objectively observe what's going on for you* or another person, *over there.* Seeing yourself playing out in the scene, as opposed to being in it. The distance will reduce the intensity of feelings. For example, years ago I opened my Filofax to find a big hairy spider. My immediate reaction was to chuck the Filofax across the room. That distance decreased my *yuk* feelings.

That distance and being able to tune into the facts of a matter will help to reduce any feelings. I find the Crow's Nest position helps me to deal with situations where I need to be able to be more objective and set my feelings to one side, (if they're preventing me from achieving an objective).

ACTION:

- Use your Crow's Nest position to remain objective, if you become consciously aware of any negative memories whilst reading this book.
- If the stories, metaphors or questions trigger a childhood memory, make a note of it in *The Inner Brilliance, Outer Shine Journal.* This will save you work later when you get to Chapter 6. Then forget about it.

At this stage, avoid taking a deep dive into your Baggage, (which incidentally we all have, which will become apparent later on), because if you allow yourself to access your past and begin over-analysing it, you will begin to re-experience old feelings as the connected neurons where the memories are encoded, begin to fire. If you do this, you run the risk of making yourself miserable. You will be able to offload any unwanted Baggage in Chapter 6.

Alternatively, if you do find yourself getting drawn into thinking about upsetting memories, do what parents do to distract a toddler who is 'stuck in state', distract yourself. Move your body. Change the environment. Focus on something different. If all else fails, tell the thought to stop and skip forward to Chapter 6 and learn how to use Havening now.

One of the best things about qualifying as a Coach was the realisation that work-life didn't have to be a certain way. I could chart my own course. I could be the Captain. But as we all know, sailing to new undiscovered territories requires bravery.

Victim, Persecutor or Brave Captain?

Another thinking trap we can fall into is getting stuck in victim mode. Victims wait to be rescued and are persecuted by their problems – things which they believe they have no control over. It's like the sheep near where we live. They learn to stay stuck in the field as a result of getting an electric shock from the fence as lambs. That electric shock teaches them to stay trapped in the field as adults, even when the fence isn't switched on or is broken. They give up trying to make a bid for freedom because they hold the same beliefs.

We too can be like sheep believing that we are stuck with our lot in work-life, incapable of change. However, science tells us that we can re-wire our brain which is continually responding to our environment, physiology, emotions and lifestyle.[16] This theory is referred to as neuroplasticity.

Add to the fact that we can even alter how our genes are expressed, by changing our thoughts, feelings, beliefs, and our environment. So, in other words, it is not a given that we will get cancer, it is whether this gene is switched on by our actions. This is according to the science of epigenetics, based on research conducted by Bruce Lipton.[17]

Another way we stay stuck is by turning into a persecutor, blaming everyone and everything else for our misery. However, both victim and persecutor positions can be comforting, though can't they? We don't have to take responsibility for what's going on around us or the results we are getting. We don't have to take constructive corrective action. We're either too busy feeling helpless and paralysed or defending and fighting our corner.

I once worked with a lady called Kirsty who was clinically depressed. In fact, in my first meeting with her she told me that if things didn't improve in her work-life, she intended to take a hot bath with some razor blades. She spoke non-stop for an hour and a half. Her story was well versed and familiar to her.

I had been warned when I was trained as a coach that clients can sometimes get *stuck in their story.* She admitted that counsellors had previously terminated their arrangements with her. I was quick to clarify that I wasn't a counsellor, that I was a coach and that coaching required action and choosing to do something different.

Several meetings in with my client Kirsty, I realised I was stuck in the Karpman Drama Triangle. There are three positions: Victim, Persecutor and Rescuer. My client was the Victim and I was the Rescuer.[18]

When she arrived for her session, I adopted a less sympathetic approach and became more business-like. I went straight into reviewing her actions so that I could establish what she was doing for herself, to change the results she was getting in work-life. I was also assessing whether coaching continued to be appropriate or if she needed to be seen by someone else.

She picked up on my state change and immediately threw her head into her hands, grabbed a tissue, and declared that she had not had a moment to herself. She said, 'As you can probably see I'm feeling very upset right now.'

I described the Karpman Drama Triangle theory and where I thought she was at – stuck in Victim. I tried to explain that if I continued to rescue her, I was helping to enable her victim-like behaviours and that I wanted her coaching sessions to be different and not like her counselling. Her body shifted again. She gripped the arms of the chair, leant forward and said in a snarling tone, 'You are not helping me! Coaching isn't working! I'm going to seriously consider whether I come back.'

This time I felt unnerved. She'd become the Persecutor. She didn't want to take alternative action and was blaming me for the lack of results she was getting.

Doing something different requires bravery and for us to become the Brave Captain of our Ship.

I had always wanted to run my own business. Whilst I was training to be a coach, all my contemporaries on the course were busy setting up their companies. I was waiting for that 'confident moment'. Two years passed. Granted I was building up coaching experience whilst I worked in HR but I didn't have the guts to take the plunge. I had all sorts of limiting beliefs as to why I couldn't run a business. I was a complete misery at home. My husband would dread asking me how my day had gone. I would launch into everything that was wrong about work, (I too would switch between victim and persecutor).

Bravery takes risk and uncomfortable feelings. Kirsty wrote to me after her coaching sessions ended. She said that the uncomfortable conversation we had at the start of our relationship, was the conversation that turned her work-life around. As Susan Jeffers said in the title of her book, you must *Feel the Fear and Do It Anyway*.

ACTION:

Where, when and with whom are you a:

- Victim?
- Persecutor?
- Brave Captain?
- Where and when is there scope for you to be braver?
- What would you like to be able to do, if you knew you wouldn't fail?

But I was a Victim

I hear you. I have heard some terrible stories from adults about their childhoods. I had some tough things to deal with myself personally, but I got over them and now I lead my best possible life both from a work and personal perspective. I am so grateful. I've made it my mission to help other people do the same. I would love to help you.

I've listened to stories which have (secretly) made me feel so upset and cross on my clients' behalf, to think of the suffering they went through. These stories have ranged from a parent who beat his child up for not winning a street fight. He was 6 years old. The fear that experience instilled in the little human being, followed him into adulthood. He was afraid of any male authority figures and would shake and sweat profusely when triggered. It held him back. That was until he let go of this through Havening and adopted the thinking strategies that follow in Chapter 8. He was dedicated to his *project me time*. Now his career is skyrocketing, and he has been promoted twice. I feel so proud on his behalf.

I've worked with adults that felt ashamed and to blame for sexual abuse they experienced as a child and were so scared that they were unable to tell anyone about it. As adults they used the only strategy, they knew would keep them safe – control. But it became exhausting for them, having to be in charge of everything and keep themselves busy so that their minds didn't wander off to those painful memories. Of course, they missed the joy of work-life. There was no headspace for it.

Then there are those at the other end of the trauma spectrum who simply felt mistreated as children. They were shamed, bullied, made to feel like a fool by teachers, friends, siblings, parents or family members.

These experiences leave a lasting imprint and can create drag on our Ship, because they weigh us down, particularly when we are re-triggered in adulthood. My clients are often completely unaware of the childhood experience which created the limiting belief, behaviour or emotion until I repeat the specific words they have used. Hence the need for *The Inner Brilliance, Outer Shine Journal* to capture your thoughts and language. Havening will help deal with these experiences and lighten your load in Chapter 6.

We can continue to blame our parents or any anyone else that was involved in those negative experiences, but all we are doing is hurting ourselves. Each time we think about those memories or find evidence which proves we aren't enough, (because that's what most limiting beliefs boil down to), it's the equivalent of going to the gym and lifting weights to build a muscle. The neural pathway of competence, (we can become very competent at not believing in ourselves) gets stronger and stronger. Not to mention all the negative chemicals we create by having those thoughts which then rush around our body and make us feel bad.

Project Me Time

Sadly, nobody can make this change happen except for you. I often say to my clients, 'If I could wave a magic wand and fix this for you, I would.' It is time to dedicate time to yourself! I refer to this as *project me time*. If you find yourself objecting to this either because it feels selfish or you can't spare the time, why are you reading this book? This is me with my bad cop hat on.

Are you hoping that change will happen through osmosis? You know, if I sleep next to this book, the change will leap off the pages and permeate my being. I find it so frustrating when people continue to complain about their work-lives and yet put zero effort into changing it. When we've got a problem we can:

- **Put up and shut up.** Don't be fooled. This requires effort. It means accepting our situation along with all our accompanying feelings and *choosing* not to do anything about it. We also have to stop torturing other people's ears with our broken record and recognise when we are stuck in Groundhog Day.
- **Move away from a problem by changing our circumstances**, e.g. get a new job.
- **Consciously change our behaviour**, e.g. stop saying yes when we really mean no, to prevent the work from piling up.
- **Get rid of our inner triggers** using Havening or EFT so that our outer response changes.

All of the above options require action on your part. You need to choose what you are going to do differently because eventually, those around you begin to get empathy fatigue.

Oprah Winfrey once said that people can be divided into two categories. They're either a 'drain' or a 'radiator'. Drains are people that make you feel negative and drained of energy having spent time with them. Radiators on the other hand make you feel fabulous because they radiate positivity and joy.

When I qualified as a coach, I was encouraged to limit time spent with drains and expand the time spent with radiators. We become the average of the five people we spend most of our time with. Don't become that person that people start to avoid and as Zig Ziglar said, 'The problem with pity parties is very few people come, and those who do, don't bring presents.'

Right, back to being good cop. I will be your cheerleader, your confidante (through *The Inner Brilliance, Outer Shine Journal*). I want you to succeed, do well, and experience the joy of work-life.

It is time to put your own buoyancy aid on, not everyone else's. You'll be no good to anyone if you don't take care of yourself. At the peak of my ME symptoms, I can remember watching my husband with our daughter on his shoulders dance around the living room to their favourite song. I hadn't had enough energy that day to get dressed, let alone dance! I knew at that point that I had to make changes to my work-life if anything for them. This helped me to re-frame my *project me time*.

ACTION:

For your *project me time*, you need a dedicated space to carry out the activities in this book – it helps if you can make it an official, tangible 'thing'. Here are some suggestions:

1. I'm hoping by now you have downloaded my free *Inner Brilliance, Outer Shine Workbook*, which includes all the activities. You can find it here: https://www.beee. company/resources

2. Alternatively, you could dedicate a brand new notebook or folder to the activities.

3. Or you could open a file note on your phone if you're more of an on-the-move type reflector.

4. Finally, identify when specifically, you are going to have *project me time*, e.g. each morning at 7.30 am – 8.00 am. You will increase your chances of success, the more specific you are about an action.

If you don't reserve a point during the day to do this, your time will get swallowed up by other activities – especially if you are a workaholic! Also, studies show that when you are looking to introduce a new habit, it can be useful to attach it to an existing one. For example, when I began reading books, I attached it to my first coffee of the morning routine.

Summary of Key Points:

- Standing on your Bridge of awareness of what's happening now and coming off autopilot is the first step towards being the Captain of your Ship.
- Flick that switch! Rather than using your Autopilot 99% of the time, become more consciously aware of the unconscious programmes that are operating. What limiting beliefs, behaviours and emotions are driving you? Be the Captain. Take charge of that 5% of conscious thought. Begin steering your Ship.
- Start tuning into the internal and external information received by your Bridge. This will inform your Captain and prevent you from crashing on the rocks, by taking alternative action.
- Use the Crow's Nest position if you catch yourself getting absorbed into negative experiences in your past. Make a note of any memories in *The Inner Brilliance, Outer Shine Journal* and then move on. Don't analyse. You can deal with these experiences in subsequent chapters.
- Recognise when you are being persecutor or victim of your problems. Save yourself and be the Brave Captain in your own journey.
- Finally, when specifically, during the day are you going to focus on *project me time*?

Chapter 3

Antidote #3: Understand What Causes You to Sink

Show me someone who has done something worthwhile, and I'll show you someone who has overcome adversity.
Lou Holtz

The purpose of the Havening work that I do with my clients, (which you will come onto in Chapter 6) is to remove the traumas that are holding them back from shining, whether big or small. In my experience, the fewer traumas a person has on board their vessel, the more inclined they are to stay afloat and be resilient to the storms that work-life can throw at us. In this chapter, we will begin to explore what trauma is and how it influences your personality, which includes your imposter syndrome thoughts and workaholic habits. You will also start to make the connections with the past experiences which are currently dulling your shine – the inner stuff affecting your outer stuff, i.e. the results you are getting. Finally, you will zero in further on your current coordinates – where you are right now.

Nature Versus Nurture Model of Personality

One of the questions I am often asked by my coachees' sponsor is, 'How long will it take for you to fix them?' I will say, that depends on what I find. What I mean by this is, the amount of 'work' required is determined by what the client has in their personal history. In Chapter 6, we will look at your ACE, (Adverse Childhood Experiences) score, which will give you a measure of how much major trauma you have had to deal with and the impact this has on health and wellbeing.

In the Havening community, we talk about big and little traumas. Examples of big trauma could include the loss of a parent, a serious illness or accident as a child. Smaller traumas might include not being picked for the football or rounders team which made you feel not good enough or feeling the shame of answering a question wrong at school. All of that said, the meaning of the event is in the eye of the beholder. These 'smaller' events could be big traumas for some individuals.

So how do these events influence our personality? Morris Massey, a marketing professor/sociologist and producer of training videos was named as one of the 27 most influential workplace experts of the time.[19] His research identified that there are three major periods a person will go through during personality formation from ages 0 – 21. Throughout this time, as a result of significant emotional events, our personality, values and beliefs are formed. We'll look at values in more detail in Chapter 4.

Nature

Some aspects of our personality are genetically encoded in our DNA. For example, my brother is 14 years younger than me and we've never lived in the same household. I would describe my brother as a highly creative, cool skateboarding daredevil dude and talented artist. As a teenager, he routinely had a limb in plaster and I suspect he now sets off metal detectors all over the place.

At my Dad's wedding reception I was having afternoon tea and my brother was sat opposite me: I felt like Miss Stiff Knickers; comfortable in the corporate world, inept and tongue-tied when it came to art-speak, dressed in my formal linen wear. We are opposites. When I talk to my brother, in my head I look and sound like Kevin Patterson the teenage character created and played by the British comedian, Harry Enfield. I am so uncool. Anyway, I'm chatting away in my awkward style, when

I notice that we are holding our teacups in the same way – with our little pinkie sticking out at a right angle.

That wasn't a nurture thing. I certainly don't recall, nor could I imagine our Dad delivering table etiquette lessons. It's genetics. At some level, we are built similarly.

Nurture - Imprint Phase

Based on Morris Massey's research, the most important time in any person's life is during the ages of 0-7. We refer to this as the 'Imprint Phase'. Our personality development is influenced by those that nurture us during this period. This could be parents, carers, grandparents, siblings, teachers, friends – basically anyone in our life during that period.

At this age (0-7), we believe whatever we are told; we have not yet developed our conscious analytical mind and therefore don't challenge the things that are communicated or the way we are being treated. Believing in Santa Claus is a great example of this. We absorb what we are told like a sponge, without questioning whether it is true or not. If a teacher is having a bad day and tells you (with an accompanying bad mood, which triggers your fight or flight system), that you are 'rubbish at spelling', that belief becomes encoded as the truth – regardless of any other prior or future facts, for example, like the day you did get 10/10 for your spelling test. These events create our map of the world – how we experience reality from *our* perspective.

What we see, hear, feel, taste and smell, is processed through our 'filters' which create *our reality*. Our filters are our values, beliefs and experience. We delete (get rid of), distort (change the meaning) and generalise (put things in boxes), based on what we have experienced before. So, if you came to believe that you were 'rubbish at spelling', as a result of that one event, which made you feel embarrassed and not good enough, every time you get a word wrong, that experience goes through your filters and is generalised into the box of 'here's another example of me being rubbish at spelling' or 'I'm not good enough'. All the positive learning occasions where you got things right being conveniently deleted.

Therefore, you need to be able to 'un-delete' things that you do well; to acknowledge not deny your Treasure Trove of gifts and talents. When you start the Havening work, you will be adjusting and, in some cases, removing any filters that are dulling your shine and getting in the way of where you want to get to.

Safe and Stable or Unsafe and Unpredictable?

Between the ages of 0-7, we are learning about for example whether the world is a safe and stable place or not? For example, did you have to deal with unexpected or dramatic change such as divorce or relocating to another area?

I have heard many adult stories, where they did not feel safe growing up. One client observed his father beating his mother up. There was constant tension in the household. He said, 'I never knew what was going to happen next.' This fear followed him into his adult life to the C-suite. He was constantly on edge, waiting for a fight to erupt. This made him difficult to be around because he was habitually tense, on edge and augmentative both as a colleague and at home.

Once the triggers were Havened away, people said he'd 'mellowed'. He retained the ability to tackle tough issues but was less emotive when doing so. He also said he felt 'like himself'. This was because his limiting beliefs, behaviours and feelings had been dissipated by Havening the source events in his childhood.

Often clients report feeling more like themselves and that's because they've offloaded the Baggage that was weighing them down. Patterns and programs of behaviour that were meant to help us survive initially, which have become outdated. It's like pressing the factory reset button on your phone, getting rid of all that unnecessary data so that it works more efficiently.

Loved or Rejected?

During the imprint period age 0-7 we are learning in our childhood relationships whether we are we loved, liked, cared for, cherished or rejected. If you weren't made to feel special growing up, or perhaps you were ignored what conclusion did you come to? Were you made to feel like a worthwhile person? For example, sometimes parents can connect with another child more, simply because they can relate to a nature aspect of their personality. Again, I have Havened countless client memories relating to parents spending more time with one child, because of a hobby. The other child takes this to mean that they are not loved as much as their sibling; that they are not good enough. These strong emotional experiences and beliefs then continue to weigh us down, unconsciously, and every time the adult is reminded, they are not loved / liked / cared for / cherished / good enough they re-trigger the old feelings from childhood.

Success or Failure?

Then we turn to our capabilities and reputation. Can we do the things that everyone else can do or are we different? What are we known for? Class clown, brainbox or something else? Are we succeeding or failing? We begin to form our identity around what we are capable of and how we are perceived. The experiences we have typically at school or during our recreational time can influence this.

I was branded a 'slow learner'. I can remember being 'sat on't thick table' as Peter Kay once described in a sketch. I'm sure he described my table! I was with the kids that backfired endless noxious onion gasses, sat in yesterday's clothing, which they'd slept and peed in the night before, (as an adult it breaks my heart to think about the neglect this child must have been experiencing) and bathed in and drank goats milk, (the child's parents were clearly innovators when you consider all the food intolerances there are today). I was the weird kid in hand-me-down clothes, with no Dad at home. Divorce wasn't the done thing back then. I was confused by the situation, there was no big departure with suitcases underarm, so I told people he'd been taken away by the fire brigade. The teacher called my mum into school.

We were all part of a special needs group. Being part of this group didn't make me feel *special*; it made me feel separate from the rest of the class. The mature adult in me would say that at least I belonged somewhere. Taken off for extra lessons in various parts of the school. The teachers' staff room was my favourite. It was in the attic of the school building and you got to it via a painted shiny black stone staircase – it was like making an ascent to the heavens and both fascinating and terrifying.

There were casual low rise, brown public authority looking chairs, arranged in a horseshoe. The room was filled with cigarette smoke and interesting bits of chatter about the school and pupils – I'm sure this is where my fascination in people began. I used to get seated up to a Formica bench which overlooked the school playground, where it seemed everyone else was out playing. Instead of focusing on the extracurricular activity, I'd either be daydreaming or earwigging. Consequently, I never won any awards for academic achievement! What I know now though is that I hadn't hit on what I was naturally good at. More on that in Chapter 4.

Nurture - Modelling Phase

Around age 8 the child begins to question the world around them – hence the dissipation of their belief in Santa. Ages 8-13 is called the Modelling Phase where the child copies the behaviours of people they admire. You may have seen children pretending to be a teacher or repeating phrases used by their parents. You may have heard your parents say, 'Do as I say, not as I do.'

I can remember a client telling me about their daughter. She'd announced that she was sat next to 'the most popular girl in the school'. My client's heart sank because they'd heard some unsavoury stories about this girl from the other school mums. They'd also seen how she operated; she'd draw the innocent in with flattery, then turn the tables.

All of a sudden her 10-year-old was taking a keen interest in the way she looked and what she wore for school. Then one evening whilst she was propped up in bed following her bedtime story, she burst into tears. She said, 'Natalie said my eyebrows look like slugs, my dress is tight and that I am a slat. What's a slat, mummy?' That's not a typo. Funnily enough, my client didn't tend to use words like slag or slut (whichever word it was meant to be), but here was her daughter expanding her vocabulary and being influenced by someone she barely knew.

Nurture - Socialisation Phase

The final stage of personality development in this model is called the 'Socialisation Phase', (ages 14-21). This is when we are influenced primarily by our friends. You hear of teenagers, 'getting in with the wrong crowd' and doing whatever the rest of their friends are doing, such as underage drinking, wearing a particular brand of clothing or liking certain genres of music etc.

I have evidence of my socialisation phase tattooed on my rear. Bizarrely it's of a bumblebee and hadn't realised I'd branded myself with my company name until several years in business. To be honest it looks more like a bespectacled alien. I had it done following a drunken night out with my tattooed boyfriend – I know, very original.

The incident took place in a seedy parlour in Morecambe. I had to kneel over an orange plastic chair. Partway through I can remember thinking *what am I doing*? My mum went mental when I got home telling me that 'tattoos are for rough people', (they weren't the pieces of art they are today). It was out of character for me. I was experimenting. I forget it's there most of the time and I suppose I could get it removed, but it serves as a reminder of my wilder days.

ACTION:

So, as you read the last few pages, did the stories, metaphors or questions trigger any childhood memories? Go back to the Crow's Nest position. Make a note of them in *The Inner Brilliance, Outer Shine Journal*. You can note both positive and negative memories – it's the negative ones which you'll be able to work on later in Chapter 6, but for now, once recorded, put them to one side. Avoid analysing, brooding or ruminating over what happened, it will only make you feel bad. Feel free to get lost in the positive ones though as they will make you feel good!

- My Imprint Phase, Age 0-7 memories include:
- My Modelling Phase, Age 8-13 memories include:
- My Socialisation Phase, Age 14-21 memories include:
- The events / memories which contributed towards me becoming a workaholic include:
- The events / memories which created my imposter syndrome include:

When Faking it Doesn't Help You Make it

Many self-help books will share strategies to help you learn to manage limiting beliefs, behaviours and feelings...put up with them. Fake it till you make it and all that jazz. I've used such a strategy (and believe it can be helpful) but ended up exhausting myself because there was too much stuff to fake; too many thoughts to squash or let go of.

The good news is that there's an opportunity to 'cheat' and re-wire your brain so that the old patterns don't recur. To prevent the daily grind of fighting inner stuff so that you shine naturally... without thinking. More about this in Chapter 6.

I was reminded recently what a mess I used to be as we flew to Crete. I'd spent many years trying to 'manage' my anxiety. It was an endless losing battle trying to talk myself out of feeling anxious. I couldn't enjoy what was right in front of me because I'd be so incapacitated by my limiting beliefs, behaviours and feelings.

I can remember taking a flight as a young adult to the Canaries at a point in my life when I had panic attacks. I was wedged between two girlfriends as they chatted merrily oblivious to my ongoing panic. I felt so embarrassed that I had panic attacks. The only person that knew about them was my mum, so I was on my own when it came to this attack. No sympathetic voice to calm me down. I felt claustrophobic – like the space on the plane was closing in on me, and then the person in front reclined his seat. Even less room to breathe. I kept imagining myself running for the exits like some crazy lady demanding that they make an emergency landing because I felt like I was going to die. Added to the fact I was convinced the plane was going to crash. I was a mess.

The thing with panic is you can't seem to regulate your breath, which in turn exacerbates things physiologically. Your pulse quickens. Your palms go sweaty. Then you start to feel dizzy and nauseous because you've upset the natural balance of oxygen and carbon dioxide. I kept thinking where's my paper bag to puke and / or breathe into. That was the mental health solution in the 90s – beta-blockers and a brown paper bag. I only took the tablets once as they made me feel worse. I spent the whole flight managing the rise and fall of panic, sat, squashed in my seat going from white to red interchangeably.

ACTION:

- Where, when and with whom are you faking it and not making it?

When Inner Stuff Dulls Your Shine

On my continued quest to 'manage' myself, I went on a meditation course. It was all the rage. Every business was running internal mindfulness courses as a one size fits all cure for stress, so I thought I ought to get with the programme.

I stuck out like a sore thumb in class. I'd missed the memo about the standard attire being sweatpants and a baggy top. I attended the workshop in between clients, so was dressed in my usual corporate uniform, (Miss Stiff Knickers made an appearance again). I was invited to kneel on the floor with the rest of the group but chose to stay perched on my chair. My dress was too tight anyway.

I bought into a good chunk of what I was taught, (in fact, I will be talking about the benefits of meditation in Chapter 10) my only reservation was that the teachers didn't look congruent with their product, which meant to me that at some level the techniques weren't fully working. They all looked as though anger was simmering beneath the surface. Whilst they were giving it ommmnn, and using their happy-clappy Rod, Jane and Freddy from *Rainbow* (an 80s kids TV programme) voices, I'm waiting for the lead instructor to explode like in the movie *Anger Management*, (where Adam Sandler goes to see his childhood nemesis monk friend at the temple and a fight erupts between them).

Towards the end of the course, I decided to get something off my chest. I asked why they didn't get rid of the thought trigger, to stop it from arising in the first place using a technique like EFT, (I hadn't learnt Havening at that stage). One delegate jumped to the teachers' defence and started slapping her forehead, 'Oh you mean like angry tapping. Yeah sure that'll work!'

Oh dear, nobody likes a smart Alec. The sweat-pant brigade turned and glared at me from the floor. I'd broken the cardinal sin of the group, I'd dared to challenge the teacher. The instructor had a mini internal explosion; brief ripples of anger wafting across her face. The tell-tale vein pounding on her forehead. I didn't fit here, but that was OK. I made my exit.

ACTION:
- What inner stuff is dulling your shine?

Cheating Change

The flight to Crete? Wonderful. No longer claustrophobic or worrying about the plane crashing. Excited to be going on holiday. Sucking up the reality of being with my beautiful family. Not an anxious thought in sight. Able to be in what I was in as opposed to being consumed by limiting beliefs, behaviours and feelings. This wasn't something I had to think through to make it happen. It occurred because I'd got rid of the triggers using Havening. That's why it feels like cheating!

If you're wondering what the trigger was, in the 70s when you stayed away from home with your baby, you didn't have all the paraphernalia that's available today, you simply pulled out a drawer halfway out and made your baby's bed in there. My memory of this was crystal clear. It was like being in a coffin, with the frame of the chest close to my face. It felt high up and like I was going to fall out because the drawer was slanted at a 25 degree angle. This is where I learnt to be claustrophobic and have a fear of heights. I was safe. I didn't fall out. I'd simply attached an unhelpful meaning to the experience.

Outdated Beliefs and Coping Strategies

Sometimes as children, we come to the wrong conclusions about things because we keep our thoughts in our heads or there isn't anyone around to give us that adult perspective and reasoning. The problem with this though is that the limiting behaviour, belief and feeling is set up for life, particularly if it occurs in that impressionable stage age 0-7 of personality formation. These events are typically one moment in time. They are not who we are and yet they can define us, right through adulthood unless we learn to let them go.

If you are a parent, give the gift of *present listening*. Allowing your child to talk in a safe and non-judgemental space, where they're not made to feel silly can help them make sense of their thoughts and feelings. One of the traits I notice in my clients is that they weren't listened to growing up. They then end up in my office expressing thoughts and feelings which should have been aired long ago.

As a result of these intense emotional childhood experiences, we develop coping strategies, so that we avoid re-experiencing the bad feeling. Take for example the Director who was told off at school for making a mistake. He'd misheard the teacher's instruction and drew in his reading book as opposed to his exercise book. He was made to stand at the front of the class, with his hands on his head. At that moment he felt intense public humiliation and shame.

The limiting belief which was born out of this was: I get things wrong. The limiting behaviour (strategy) that was created was: I must get everything right and I mean everything! He had multiple to-do lists so that nothing got missed, including one which listed routine tasks such as: put petrol in the car, mow the lawn, take the dog for a walk.

These coping strategies are fine, provided they are effective. The constant listing of things to do was stressing him out – and I am an advocate of to-do lists but as with most things, everything in moderation.

The other downside of coping strategies and trying to manage our way around bad feelings is that we can't control when we are triggered. I was coaching this gentleman because he'd reached a tipping point when at a recent quality audit at work, his department had been marked down for a minor non-compliance. He'd got something wrong in his mind. This was fed back at a board meeting and the poor chap was re-triggered into feeling that same public humiliation and shame, he experienced as a 5-year-old boy in the classroom.

If we remove the trigger using Havening, we remove the need to adopt a coping strategy. In some circumstances, we can simultaneously remove the limiting belief, behaviour and feeling.

ACTION:

- What coping strategies do you use to avoid negative feelings?
- What are those feelings?
- When did they start?

One of the benefits of adversity is that we learn great skills. This client had learnt to be super-organised and chose a career in compliance so that he wouldn't be at risk of getting things wrong. I'm often asked am I going to stop being good at, in his case, being organised, if I get rid of the trigger? In my experience, you'll always be able to access the skills, the difference will be that you will no longer feel a compulsion to behave in a limiting way (in his case over-doing the to-do list to feel safe, relaxed and not at risk of making a mistake); it will become a choice.

Snapshot

I see the majority of my coaching clients from my home office. When I open my front door, unconsciously I am taking a mental snapshot of how the client is. Are they better, worse or about the same?

If we work on the premise that state of mind drives our behaviour, for example, if I'm in an anxious state of mind whilst presenting this could damage my performance as a Trainer; state of mind becomes important. Similarly, if you're a salesperson and you're feeling depressed it could make it difficult to enthusiastically sell your product or service, resulting in a poor sales performance.

When I'm taking a snapshot of my client, I am checking out how they are holding themselves both in their torso but primarily in their face, (their outer stuff). Our body language and how we speak expresses what we are really thinking and feeling at an unconscious level, (our inner stuff). For example, if I wanted to finish a conversation my body might begin leaning towards the door and my speech become more clipped.

When I begin working with a client I ask them to write down a snapshot of where they are at now – their Position A. I ask for a warts and all account. I want to know what are the limiting beliefs, behaviours, and feelings which are holding them back. What's dulling their shine? I ask them to tell me exactly as it is; to avoid filtering. This is their first set of coordinates. I do this because unless we get to the truth of what's happening right now, how can we begin to solve it? How do we know what we need to journey away from? This is where your Bridge of self-awareness is useful again.

ACTION:

The activity below can be repeated for up to three different contexts.

Snapshot – Your Position A:
- Pick an area of your work-life that you would like to change as part of this book.
- What habits or behaviours would like to change within your chosen context?
- When do these behaviours occur? Provide some examples.
- What feelings do you experience in this context?
- What do you believe about yourself / others in this situation?
- How does this development area impact your work-life?

- How long have you had this limiting belief, behaviour or feeling? *What's your earliest recollection of this, (ideally age 0-7)?

*If any memories pop up, make sure you use the Crow's Nest position. Stay objective and distant from the memory. Avoid analysing or ruminating. Make a note of it in *The Inner Brilliance, Outer Shine Journal* and save it for the Havening Chapter, where you will be able to 'erase' it.

Reality Check

I am not going to get all Rod, Jane and Freddie on you, promising a panacea for every single limiting belief, behaviour and feeling. Emotions serve a purpose, as I will explain in Chapter 9. They drive action and help us experience the light and shade of life. For example, it's not that you'll never experience anger, but responding to your colleagues free of the compulsion to behave in a brusque or timid way, could become reality for you, provided you can get to the original trigger in your childhood.

Also, I don't believe in being on a never-ending quest for perfection – that's damaging, hopeless and unsatisfying. I tend to get rid of whatever is getting in the way of me journeying to my current destination, (I'll be coming onto goals and vision in Chapter 5) and make a course change in the right direction. Then, when I set a new destination, which presents new challenges, I reapply the techniques within that context. Not having to be the perfect article is both freeing and exciting to me. Imagine what else we are all capable of, in this voyage of discovery we call life!

That said if you were to Haven a significant number of negative memories from your childhood. You will feel different. You will begin to feel more like the real you.

The Inner Brilliance, Outer Shine Journal

As part of this process, it would be helpful if you could begin journaling. You can download *The Inner Brilliance, Outer Shine Journal* here: https://www.beee.company/resources . We will be looking at this in more detail in Chapter 8. Some of my clients bring me their journal each month and we work through all the situations when they have been triggered emotionally, i.e. with something that has caused them to ruminate or react in a limiting way.

In the early days, it can be tricky for some, detecting what needs to be worked on, because they are still on Autopilot and not yet tuned into the information coming in on their Bridge. If you have the luxury of either a Fitbit or some other wearable technology which can measure your pulse, you can spot when you have been triggered emotionally.

I was working with a gentleman who wasn't quite accepting that he'd been triggered in a board meeting. It was the first thing he told me about during his session – this is important from a coaching perspective because often clients can't get on and do the work during a session until they get the thing that is troubling them the most off their chest.

I asked him how he felt about what his colleague had said to him; he'd accused him of being insensitive with an employee. His response, 'not bothered.' Whilst he said this, he began jaw-bunching. His body was telling me otherwise. This was a guy who preferred hard tangible evidence. None of that gut feeling, mumbo jumbo, ethereal stuff. I asked him if I could see what his heart rate was during the meeting. He physically shrank in his chair. When we viewed the report it looked as if he was sprinting. Now he was ready to talk. No longer stuck in denial.

ACTION:

The Inner Brilliance, Outer Shine Journal

For now, simply start writing down your thoughts, feelings and reflections of the day in *The Inner Brilliance, Outer Shine Journal*. Don't re-read what you have written, until you are instructed to take another look. The purpose is to download and process what is in your head; to de-stress and make you feel a little lighter, but ultimately to make your life easier when you use Havening in Chapter 6.

- To begin with, reflect over the last 7-28 days and make a note in *The Inner Brilliance, Outer Shine Journal* of the situations where you were triggered negatively, emotionally. Identify where, when and with whom this occurred. What were the limiting beliefs, behaviours and feelings at play?
- If any memories pop up which you feel may require Havening, simply put an 'H' in the margin, so that you can quickly find it when you need it.
- Going forward, use *The Inner Brilliance, Outer Shine Journal* daily to note any subsequent triggers, thoughts, feelings and reflections.
- Start to spot any limiting belief, behaviour or emotion in your text and highlight them. This will be useful when you start your havening work; it can feel like being a detective, making sense of all the clues from your language, so that you can identify what to go after.
- Alternatively, if you own wearable technology such as a Fitbit, you could look at your beats per minute to identify when you may have been triggered emotionally. It usually looks like you were running a race, when in fact you know you were sat stationary.

Finally, when I'm working with clients sometimes, they will say, 'I had a wonderful childhood and my parents were good people.' I get that entirely. I am a parent and I hope that our child would show us the same loyalty.

Parenting is both the toughest and most magical job. Whilst you're with them you're 'in-role' the whole time. Every little behaviour and feeling being observed and logged away for a later date. It is the most important role you can play (in my humble opinion), in the development of any human being.

Doing the work I do with clients has made me a paranoid parent; I can see all the opportunities for screwing our daughter up. We are by no means perfect. Our daughter is very self-aware and will openly tell us when we do, along with all the other human beings that have come into contact with her. This is because what excites or makes one person laugh, can cause minor (or major) trauma in others.

For those of you that think your parents or carers were crap, I hear you too.

Summary of Key Points:
- The more Baggage we have on board as a result of minor or major trauma, the more at risk we are of sinking.
- Offloading Baggage using Havening can make you more resilient.
- Use the Crow's Nest to stay objectively removed from your Baggage. Taking a deep dive into Baggage without applying a technique can make you feel crappy.
- Start using *The Inner Brilliance, Outer Shine Journal* to note when you experience any limiting beliefs, behaviours or feelings.
- Our personality is a mix of both nature (things that are genetically encoded) and nurture. We can change the limiting nurture aspects of our personality using Havening.
- Relax and be easy, most human beings have some Baggage, it's part of the nurture aspect of our personality.

Chapter 4

Antidote #4: Align Towards Your Stars

If you deliberately plan on being less than you are capable of being, then I warn you that you'll be unhappy for the rest of your life.
Abraham Maslow

As I have said before, I think we all have the potential to be brilliant in a job or the thing we do to earn a living, somewhere. Having worked with 1000's of people over the years, I've noticed that there is a real sweet spot when it comes to excelling in a vocation. Just as the ancient navigators used the stars to guide them on their journey, we're going to use your strengths, values and purpose, supported by empowering, affirmative beliefs, (see Chapter 8), to get you heading towards Destination Joy – summarised by a vision and goals in Chapter 5. This will enable you to shine, achieve natural success and access the joy of work-life again. Because, when we're not in that place, work can either seem like a massive drag or we feel bad about ourselves. It becomes a self-perpetuating negative downward spiral.

Have you ever worked somewhere and didn't fit in? This was probably values misalignment. Have you ever been a poor performer or done a rubbish job? This could have been strengths misalignment. Have you ever been really bored at work? My guess is you weren't being stretched enough nor working towards something where you could make a difference. This was probably purpose and goals misalignment. As someone who used to work in HR, I've seen this time and time again.

Take Thomas, an office manager. He was super-quick at his job and intelligent. This meant that he got through his workload fast. The business was under-utilising him, but that was because he had a reputation for being a troublemaker. Once he'd finished his work, he'd move from department to department spreading malicious rumours – usually about HR! He didn't like change or newcomers. The leaders despised him. He also didn't believe in himself and had so much potential. The reason he spoke so negatively about the business, is that he felt bad inside. Part of him knew he was disliked and so the downward spiral continued.

Once I spotted what was going on, I decided to take a different tack with Thomas. Whenever there was an HR project, I invited him to be on the committee. Whenever I ran a leadership development programme, I invited him to attend. Part of me recognised that this could have backfired, but I wanted to believe that he had talent and could be turned around.

He blossomed. He shone. Not only did he become a strong advocate of HR, but he also spread positive words about what the business was doing. He was influential at all levels of the organisation. Thomas was a great communicator. He was playing to his strengths but in a good way. He became aligned to his stars.

Strengths

Donald O. Clifton was an Educational Psychologist and Chair of the Gallup International Research and Educational Centre and studied what was right with people. He developed a philosophy of people achieving excellence by focussing on their strengths as opposed to improving weaknesses. As part of his research he discovered that those who received strengths feedback showed 12.5% greater productivity, turnover rates were 14.9% lower and profitability increased 8.9% in the business units they worked for, post-intervention.[20]

Learning about strengths was one of the things that propelled my career. Up until that point, it had been hit and miss in terms of what I was able to achieve, how successful I was and how happy I felt in a role. Additionally, understanding what you're good at and taking *owner-ship* of your strengths acts as an antidote to imposter syndrome. In a study, the researchers concluded that being mindful of character strengths improved psychological well-being.[21]

When Our Shine is Dulled

Growing up, my childhood friends and family would probably have described me, (if they completed an anonymous survey), as average, (notice I've gone up in the world, no longer in remedial class) shy, timid, and a bit beige; the sort of person you could ignore. I would happily blend into the fabric of any woodchip wall. Based on my past performance at school there weren't any great expectations about how I would perform academically. I can remember the look of first surprise, followed by joy on my mum's face when I and came out with 5 GCSEs at grade C or above. This was a good result for me! My first mistake: picking subjects I thought I ought to study, rather than what I enjoyed or was good at.

Consequently, I was told that my results weren't good enough for the prestigious Costa del Morecambe High School 6th Form and that I would be better suited to the college. So, off I tootle and signed up for a BTEC in Business and Finance because I thought the course title made me sound all proper – my second mistake. The bit I did get right, was following my instincts to study Human Resources because I'd always been fascinated in people, which featured as a module a few hours a week. The rest of the time my best friend and I would agree on the skiving off rota. I was bored. I had no interest in the other subject areas. I am amazed I passed.

Following the theme of being interested in people, I applied for a job as a Personnel Assistant in a factory. On the day I joined, my manager took me into what was going to be my office. It used to house the company's only computer. They were big back then. He slid the office / cupboard door shut. I knew something was up. In a hushed voice he broke the devastating news; 'I know I said you were going to work in Personnel, well, we'd like you to spend half your time in payroll.' Most HR professionals will tell you that, not only can you not do that kind of thing, you know, completely change someone's job description without consulting with them, but it's also sacrilege. People and numbers don't mix. I'm kidding. Sweeping generalisation. That's only me.

My HR boss hesitantly introduced me to my other boss, the Payroll Clerk. Her nickname was, 'The Lady in Grey' because everything about her was grey: her clothing, hair, personality and the smoke from her 60 cigarettes! I could barely see who I was being introduced to for the plumes of smoke. Everyone was frightened of her – even the burly factory operators. I saw many grown men reduced to snivelling wrecks after an incident with this lady. She had what looked like a serving hatch, which she slammed open at certain times of the day to deal with payroll queries. If a poor bloke came to complain that he'd been paid incorrectly, (usually by me), she'd practically catch their fingers in the hatch door as she slammed it shut again.

ACTION:
- When, where and with whom has your shine been dulled?
- When have you been misaligned to your strengths in a role?
- What did you think or believe about yourself in that context?
- How did this situation make you feel?

Accepting Our Nature-Based Weaknesses
As you're probably guessing, numbers are not my strong point. When people talk numbers, it sounds like blah blah blah. When I worked as the Head of HR in an open plan office, my colleagues would snigger if I tried to ring a number on hands-free. The

phone would usually say, 'This number is not recognised'. Rude. I suspect I have dyscalculia. Numbers literally jump around on the page. Another special talent!

When it came to the payroll job, there were so many things that were misaligned, but the biggest thing was my strengths. Add into the mix that I am more of a visual and kinesthetic learner. This means I need to *see* and then *do* to understand. I had to sit there for hours on end, listening to the Lady in Grey *telling* me about payroll. With hindsight, it wasn't surprising that when she went on holiday, lots of people got paid wrong. It felt like pressing a button to release the national lottery balls... only a bad lottery; I never knew what numbers were going to come out.

Failure is a good thing, provided we are developing or improving something. Repeatedly failing in a role can mean that we're simply not aligned to our strengths. We all have weaknesses and unless it is a nurture-based limitation, (which I will come on to), it can be difficult to fix.

Take Edward, an HR Director able to deliver a spontaneous speech and highly creative. He could detect and correct cultural and leadership issues in innovative ways – that's how his organisation benefited from his strengths. However, when it came to implementing policy, procedure and HR initiatives to a strict timetable, he struggled. He didn't have a natural innate ability to be organised, but it didn't matter. He had a huge team around him that could take care of that stuff. He was also brilliant in a crisis. Always a beacon of calm for the rest of the organisation. Strengths such as being creative, intuitive, spontaneous and calm were nature aspects of his personality; being organised was not.

Fixing Our Nurture-Based Weaknesses
Compare and contrast this with another client, Jo, who was also disorganised, but this was due to a nurture aspect of her

personality. She had been sent for coaching by her boss because she kept disappearing. Jo was stressed and behind with her workload. Customers were complaining about her because she would say yes to an instruction and then not deliver. When the customers chased her for an update, she'd ignore them for weeks and they'd end up calling her manager.

When I got talking to Jo, she said that once problems started, she wanted to *bury her head in the sand and run away*. This behaviour caused her to be disorganised. When I asked her whether she could remember a time in the past when she ran away from problems and buried her head in the sand, she said yes instantly.

When she was growing up there was a very public family feud which caused her parents great upset. Every time her mum got emotional about the situation, Jo would run away to her bedroom and bury her head under the duvet. She would drown out the noise from below with her headphones and read her favourite *Jackie* magazine. She said she felt helpless; that running away was her only solution.

Sadly, this strategy followed her through to her adult life. She had become like the sheep referred to in Chapter 2. Whilst she might have felt helpless as a child, and there probably wasn't a great deal she could do, that strategy had become outdated once an adult. Burying her head was making her seem disorganised.

Once we cleared up the associated events on Jo's timeline, she was able to be better organised and manage her time more effectively. She was no longer afraid to face problems and would happily call customers or drop them an email to alert them to any problems arising. This in turn stemmed the flow of complaints, enabled her to catch up with her workload and reduced her stress.

ACTION:

- What are your foibles or weaknesses – we all have them?

- When have you repeatedly failed in the same context?
- What have been your career low points? When haven't you shone?
- Which weaknesses were you trying to use?
- Which of these weaknesses were nurture based? For example, were you ever told that you couldn't do or be something, which then became a self-fulfilling prophecy? If you can find the event, make a note of it in *The Inner Brilliance, Outer Shine Journal*. Mark the memory with an 'H' in the margin as a reminder to Haven it when you get to Chapter 6.
- How can you begin to get comfortable and accept your weaknesses, without shame or judgement?
- How can you begin to learn to love your foibles; they are part of you? Even better, how can you learn to laugh at yourself (in a good way) occasionally? More about this in Chapter 8.

If you're stuck with a weakness you don't like, I've seen many authentic executives and leaders be honest about the things they don't do so well and then work around them by employing people to do the things they can't.

Alternatively, clients have taken a new direction in their career, so that they become aligned to their strengths. Martin Seligman, the father of Positive Psychology focused on how to encourage positive behaviour as opposed to how to prevent negative behaviour. He found that the most satisfied, upbeat people were those who had discovered and exploited their unique combination of signature strengths.[22]

Things reached a crescendo for me in my payroll job when having cocked up again, I was called into the Accountant's Office. He was a creepy, oily little man, that wouldn't think twice about patting your rear if you happened to be standing by the photocopier. You could always tell wherever he'd been because he'd leave a little waft of something unpleasant.

Anyway, The Lady in Grey started on her rant about all my mistakes; the Accountant was afraid of her too. Conveniently, this also sounded like blah blah blah. I zoned out temporarily until she'd finished. I'd become a problem employee; the sort who would probably be put on a performance review type thing these days. This was an old-fashioned business in the 90s though. He said, 'Pull your socks up or you're sacked.' Then he said, 'Why are your hands all shiny? Do you have glue on them?' The Accountant didn't do people, he couldn't read that I was bricking it and my hands were sweaty! I was shining in the wrong places. I thought I was going to lose my job there and then and was worried about how I would make the loan payments for my beloved green Fiat Uno.

Spotting When the Stars Align

Gradually, over the years I started to become more aligned to the things I was good at. You can do this too by:

- **Noticing what tasks you find easy and enjoyable.** Often when we are working in line with strengths, the task seems effortless. We mistakenly believe that everyone finds the activity we are engrossed in, just as easy and enjoyable. We get lost in time and enter into what sportsmen and women call a 'flow state'. For example, I am the chief organiser in my family. I love planning fun events and thinking ahead. I used to get frustrated when others didn't do the same. Now I accept it is one of my strengths. It doesn't matter that we are not the same. It's a good thing!

- **Tuning into what the personality profiles say.** When I took The Myers-Briggs Type Indicator® my boss told me that I was an introvert and more suited to a training role. I thought she was crazy at the time, (see friends / family description previously). I started out doing 20-minute toolbox talks and then before I knew it, was delivering 13-day events.

- **Taking on board what work colleagues say**. I spent three weeks in London training as an NLP (Neuro Linguistic Programming) Trainer. It was hardcore. I studied until 1 am most days and was up again ready to start at 7 am.

  The school I attended (The NLP Academy) had high standards. Not only were there exams, but you also had to be able to demonstrate the techniques in front of an audience of about 80. It was nerve-wracking stuff.

  John Grinder, the co-creator of NLP, (NLP god in my eyes) would observe and give feedback. If I said that John, before inventing NLP was a captain in the US Special Forces in Europe during the Cold War and then went on to work for a US intelligence agency, does that give you an insight into his personality?

  Whenever he spoke, it felt like you were in the presence of a genius. My imposter syndrome thoughts would go into overdrive if I conversed with him. Anyway, I finish my timeline demonstration and he said in a beautiful American drawl, 'She's one to watch.' I couldn't believe it.

  The next day I collected my delegate badge and it was covered in gold stars. When I asked why, the NLP Assessor said, 'Because you're a star.' I felt completely surprised and humbled by both comments.

- **Getting a strengths profile**. Early on in my career, I completed a profile as part of a book called *Now Discover Your Strengths*.[23] Finding this out enabled me to take advantage of my visioning strength, which I hadn't developed yet. It is now a fundamental part of my business and love working with organisations to establish their vision.

ACTION:

Time to make an entry into *The Inner Brilliance Outer, Shine Workbook*:

- What tasks do you find easy, complete in that flow state, where time passes quickly, and you experience joy?
- Reflect on what previous personality profiles have said about you. If you haven't completed one yet, consider investing in a Strengths Finder profile, which you get as part of the book I mentioned earlier, or you can buy it separately online.[24] Via offer a free strengths survey.[25] My favourite is UK based company Strengths Profile who have produced a questionnaire and book.[26] You can buy one here: https://www.beee.company/resources
- What compliments have you received when completing a task?
- What do you think your strengths are? Identify your top 5. If you're struggling with this, phone a trusted friend or family member and ask them.
- Allow yourself to notice over the next few days, what you do well. Do you remember *owner-ship* in Chapter 2? Continue to raise awareness and note your gifts, talents and achievements. They are what make you, you. Owning them will help diminish imposter syndrome thoughts.

Overdoing Strengths

One of my husband's favourite sayings is, 'Overdoing a strength can become a weakness.' Take Nigel, a busy executive who is instrumental in a creative business. Whenever his clients presented him with a problem, Nigel would happily provide a solution, regardless of the profit margin, workforce capability or capacity.

The overdone strength of creativity drives chaos in the business, which results in orders being delivered late, non-profitable products and staff being pulled in lots of different directions. The whole workforce seems stressed! Additionally, focusing on lots of things prevented the company from developing a reputation for being amazing at one thing. His strength was out of balance. Equally, we're not going to shine to our full potential if we are underdoing our strengths.

ACTION:

Using the scale below, score each of your strengths out of 10. Then having assessed each strength, identify what you could do to fully use each strength or bring them back into balance, i.e. move each strength to a 5. This may mean doing more of some things and less of others!

Underdone Strength					Balanced	Overdone Strength				
0	1	2	3	4	5	6	7	8	9	10

Strength:	Score:	What are you going to stop or start doing to bring each strength into balance?

Values

Depending on which strengths profile you complete, often there can be an overlap between a strength and a value, for example, one of my strengths is 'honesty' and there is a strong connection with my value of integrity, so as you proceed through this chapter, watch out for those connections too!

Values are the things that are important to us. When pitching for business, I routinely ask my prospective clients what is important to them about the assignment, because it helps to elicit their values for the project. It doesn't matter what's important to me at that moment, as I am not the one doing the buying, (although I will be checking that our businesses hold similar values).

For example, when buying a car we usually have a list of requirements. My list usually includes make, model, colour, price and what the drive is like. I am not interested in fancy widgets. Nor do I want to hear about what's under the bonnet. When a salesperson tries to force-feed me information that's not important, I switch off and they usually lose the sale.

We have different values in different contexts and some which run across all situations. We usually refer to these as our core values. In this book, we will be focussing primarily on your work values, but any of the exercises that follow you could apply to other contexts too if you choose.

ACTION:

- Pick a context, e.g., buying a house or choosing a partner. Now ask yourself, 'What's important to me in this context?' and identify up to 6 things. We'll explore your work-based values more, further on in this chapter.

Values Misalignment

One of the things I love about running my own business is that I can choose who I do business with and as part of that, working with companies that value integrity is important. For me, integrity means (as we all have unique definitions for words) trust, honesty and being straight forward. It's about knowing where you are with somebody.

I was engaged by an organisation to do a values-based culture change. It was quite a prestigious establishment, and this blinded me to some of the red flags and value conflicts that showed up early in the project.

Firstly, the contracting was quite lengthy, (this is the unpaid part of my work). I had numerous meetings with the board to clarify the objectives of the programme and run through how I was going to deliver things. There was what seemed like endless detail. Part of me didn't mind this, as it meant we were getting clear about expectations and outputs – knowing where we were all at. However, it was beginning to be a little excessive and was starting to err on the side of control-freakery. They wanted to know, minute by minute what I was going to be saying and doing.

During these early meetings, I explained that as part of the process we would be analysing what existing values were in place so that we didn't throw the baby out with the bathwater. This would involve speaking to the workforce, before deciding which values would support a movement towards the vision and mission. When I asked the CEO whether he would like his fellow directors to choose the future values or consult with the broader organisation, he was very clear – 'Let the workforce decide!' This was a great move because allowing the team to establish what behaviours were necessary to take the business forward, meant that not only would they engage with the project, but they would gain a deep understanding of the overall strategy.

When I reflect on those meetings, I recall listening to the CEO giving me chapter and verse on his accolades. I can remember thinking *how is this relevant to the brief?* The organisation was an interesting mix of self-important leaders and altruists. No wonder they wanted to align their culture!

When I arrived to deliver their first session, I had to wait an hour and a half before they'd let me into the room. My chaperone was insistent that I wait and speak to the Chairman before setting up. We both stood in his line of sight for 7 minutes, whilst he finished off his conversation. I was then expected to deliver my session in half the time, as they had a strict agenda to adhere to! I felt uneasy.

Feeling uneasy can be a sign that your values are misaligned.

As I began running the workshop, it was clear that the altruists weren't allowed to have an opinion. Whatever the Chairman thought, everyone else would quickly step in line and agree with him. Those that were prepared to put their head above the parapet (and these were Directors and senior leaders), were publicly shot down in flames. How were we going to ascertain which value-based behaviours needed to stay and which needed to go, if people weren't allowed to be honest?

When I finished the session, the CEO collared me and said, 'Why didn't we select the values today?' I reminded him of the detailed proposal and minute by minute account that I'd been asked to provide, and that he'd said he wanted the 'workforce to decide'.

When Negative Feelings Are a Sign of Misalignment

I felt confused. Never in all my consulting time had I been asked to provide so much detail and yet, I'd not delivered what he'd expected. He'd changed the goalposts. I realised that this had become a box-ticking exercise. Following the first session, he now understood that the team would get to be honest about what was going on in the business and he wanted to claw this back. Keeping up appearances, (hiding the truth), control and micromanaging was what was important to this business. I couldn't align with this organisation's unspoken values. I felt miserable, stressed and unsure of myself.

That's the thing with values, they can make us behave illogically because of something jarring on our conscience. They are our measure of what's right and wrong. When our values aren't met, we can feel the worst of feelings: guilt, regret, uneasiness, stress, anxiety, anger, shame etc. But ultimately like we don't belong. However, when we do get our values satisfied, we can experience the polar opposite of feelings such as joy, achievement, satisfaction, contentment, happiness etc.

ACTION:

- Which organisation(s) have you worked for where you didn't fit in or you felt uneasy?
- What feelings did you experience whilst you were working there?
- Which needs weren't being met?

Towards and Away from Values

Now, the thing about values is that we can have *towards* and *away* from values. Values are supported by a series of beliefs and are often connected with our childhood as a result of repeat conditioning or intensely positive or negative experiences. Around age 10, our core values have been formed. For example, politeness continues to be a value in my family, which was passed onto me by my mum. We were routinely reminded to say please and thank you and to wait before everyone sat down at the table before starting dinner. I have continued this tradition with our daughter. My beliefs that support politeness include:

- It doesn't cost you anything.
- Manners can let someone know how much you appreciate what the other person has done for you.
- It's a way of showing dignity and respect, regardless of the other person's position in society.
- It's rude to be impolite.
- Manners make a difference to the other person. (I feel humbled by the number of occasions we have been upgraded and received spontaneous gifts on holiday).

I would describe the above value as being *towards* something positive and as a result of repeat conditioning. Whilst there is one negative belief amongst the list, most of them are positive.

Unsurprisingly, *achievement* is one of my values, which is *away from* a lack of academic achievement. This value was created as a result of a series of negative events, which produced limiting beliefs such as:

- I am not good enough.
- I am not intelligent.
- I am a slow learner.
- I am different.

Overdoing Values

The trouble with away from values is that we can over-do these too. Take my brutally honest client, Aaron. He was a banker and in the habit of saying what he sees. Honesty became important to Aaron because he was always trapped between his divorced parents growing up. His mum would put him under pressure to deliver messages to his Dad on his weekend visits. If he didn't deliver the message, he would get his ears boxed when he returned home.

To further compound this, his Dad would get Aaron to keep secrets from his mum. Aaron's Dad wasn't into paying maintenance and didn't want his ex-wife knowing that they'd got a tan because they'd been sunning themselves in Costa del Sol. Aaron would feel stressed if he knew something and wasn't able to pass the message on.

His way of dealing with this as an adult – his coping strategy, was to relieve himself of the burden immediately blurting out what was on his mind. He was running away from getting into trouble. The way to keep the peace was for everything to be above board and transparent. However, this caused him problems in his role, as he would often say things to his clients that made them feel uncomfortable, such as 'that suit doesn't fit you properly'. He was overdoing the value of honesty.

Sometimes our values can shift overnight. Having my daughter made a big difference. When she arrived, *family* shot to the top of my list of what was important. Additionally, Havening and using EFT demoted my value of achievement, by getting rid of the negative events, which caused the limiting beliefs. For example, I was recently invited to speak at a European conference. It would have been a great profile-raising prospect. However, it was running on my daughter's birthday. I didn't have to give a second thought to decline the opportunity. Whereas the old me used to run courses at weekends.

ACTION:

Continue to complete your *Inner Brilliance, Outer Shine Workbook* by answering the following questions. You can access my *Inner Brilliance, Outer Shine Workbook* template for this activity here: https://www.beee.company/resources

- To establish what your values are, we must pick a context. For the purposes of this book, if you are going to *shine* in your occupation, what's important to you at work? What absolutely must be in place for you to be happy in a job? Make a list of up to 6 things.
- Then for each value, define what it means to you.
- Once you've got your list put them in order of priority, #1 being the most important.

Value:	Meaning:	Priority:

Next, you're going to look at where these values come from. This puts you back in the captain's seat. The more you raise awareness of who you are, the more you can choose what you do with this information and how it influences you going forward. There will also be an opportunity to haven away any negative experiences which have led to limiting beliefs in Chapter 6:

Value:	Chilhood experiences which created this value:	Beliefs associated with this value:	Is this a towards or an away from value?

When we over or under do a value, we can experience negative emotions and feelings. For example, overdoing 'achievement' could lead to workaholism and stress. Equally, underdoing 'creativity' because of imposter thoughts about not being good enough could make you feel frustrated and dissatisfied. Again, there is a sweet spot, and ideally, we want our values to be in balance.

Next, score each value using the scale below.

Now identify what you could do to get each value fully satisfied and in balance. This may mean doing more of some things and less of others!

Underdone Value					Balanced	Overdone Value				
0	1	2	3	4	5	6	7	8	9	10

Value:	Score:	What are you going to stop or start doing to bring each value into balance?

Purpose

When David Blaine was interviewed by Chris Evans on Virgin Radio and was asked how he got into magic, he said it was because of his mum. She was a single parent and so had to hold down several jobs. She gave him a pack of cards to play with, which he would take everywhere with him, but didn't know what to do with them.

One day whilst his mum was working at the library, one of her colleagues showed him a mathematical playing card trick. At the end of her shift, he demonstrated the trick to his mum, and she was completely blown away by it. He'd made his mum happy. This made him go in pursuit of further tricks, so he could continue to make her happy.

This is such a great story. David's purpose was borne out of that positive childhood experience. I have worked with clients that have experienced deep dissatisfaction with life because they've ignored their purpose.

Take Rose a teacher who chose the profession because her dad said, 'The acceptable occupations in this household include: Solicitor, Doctor, Vet, Teacher or Banker.' And yet as a child, she loved to write creatively. She knew being a writer was frowned upon, so used to make up stories by torchlight under the covers. It was only when she hit her 50's that she decided to explore her purpose further and took up a creative writing class intending to leave her teaching job.

When we work in line with purpose, we feel as though we have made a difference. My purpose is expressed in my business mission: optimising brilliance. There is nothing I love more than to see a business or individual do well. I think by this stage, you will get why this is important to me and where it stems from. When I am working in line with my purpose and I hear my clients tell me about their success stories, the hairs on my arms stand on end. I know when I'm aligned to purpose because I experience joy.

Often our purpose manifests itself as a result of our childhood experiences and has connections with our values and strengths. I see our purpose as a neat summary of these two things and as a demonstration of where we make a difference in this world.

ACTION:

To identify your purpose, answer the following questions:

- When, where and with whom have you felt like you made a difference and experienced joy? What were you doing?
- When, where and with whom have you become frustrated, disengaged or demotivated? What weren't you doing?
- When you die, what would you like your legacy to be? What would you like people to say about you?
- Now, summarise your purpose in one sentence. If you're

a reflector, write it on a post-it note and pin it somewhere you can see it. Then hone it.

- What are your thoughts and ideas about what you could do to become more aligned to your purpose?

The next part of the voyage is to decide where you're going to be taking your Ship to.

Summary of Key Points:
- Establish what your strengths are and notice and own your gifts, talents and achievements. Acknowledging strengths is good for your wellbeing and is one of the antidotes to imposter syndrome.
- Accept that we all have weaknesses; get comfortable with them.
- Remember that any strength overdone can become a weakness. Take action to bring strengths into balance.
- Recognise what's important to you in a role and if you are feeling stressed, uneasy or other negative emotions, check to see which value isn't being met. Then take action to rectify the situation.
- As with strengths, notice when you are over-doing a value and identify whether there are connections with over-working. Again, take action to bring the value back into balance.
- Your purpose can be a neat summary of your strengths, values and how you make a difference in the world. We can experience intense positive emotions and shine when we work in line with purpose.

Chapter 5

Antidote #5: Navigate to Destination Joy

A vision without action is just a dream. Action without vision is a nightmare.
Chinese Proverb

I have worked with Jennifer regularly for several years, choosing to use her sessions these days as a recap, refocus and reset. She often talks about how much she loves life during coaching. She runs a successful business, has a husband whom she adores and two great kids she's very proud of. They go on amazing holidays and live in a fantastic home. They want for nothing. So much so, that she has made many anonymous contributions to charity. She doesn't expect public recognition and only shares this in the privacy of her session with me, because it makes her happy to be able to do these things. She is very well-adjusted and thinks well of herself in an understated way. She is at 'Destination Joy'. It hasn't always been that way though. In this chapter, we look at how you too can plot your way to your version of Destination Joy.

Destination Grim

Most of us don't intentionally end up at Destination Grim. It's usually a series of small unconscious moves that take us off course and heading in the wrong direction – hence the need for coming off Autopilot and becoming your own Captain. Then we wake up one morning and think, how on earth did I end up here? The joy of work-life has gone. We're stressed, overworked and overwhelmed with everything. There's no headspace for joy.

Back to Jennifer. When I first met her, I would describe her as direct to the point of being brusque, on high alert, guarded and tense. However, I saw a chink in her armour after her team delivered a presentation following a personal development programme I'd been running. We'd spent months together and they too had been on a 'voyage'. Their presentations were heart-felt, some of them sharing how much they didn't believe in themselves before they started the course. At one point, Jennifer momentarily teared up – blink and you'd miss it. She could relate to what they were saying. She was having a crisis of confidence and belief and yet here she was, the big successful boss with a tough exterior. Nobody else knew what she was *really* feeling inside.

I shared my observations and encouraged her to book a free discovery session. It took months for her to finally come for coaching. When she did, she described her Destination Grim.

She'd got off course because one of the top jobs would soon be available and it was looking unlikely that she was going to get it. Jennifer's colleague was favoured because she was better at administering the business. This made Jennifer doubt herself. In her mind, it had always been the logical next step. However, how many people get promoted away from their strengths and damage their success and happiness?

Add to the fact that Jennifer's relationships at work were tense, as was the atmosphere at home. She couldn't switch off. She described it as a 'tension across my shoulders which is always there'. When she went on holiday, it took almost the whole vacation to switch off, let alone unwind. She couldn't be present for people. She was already a very successful woman with everything that she needed, she just wasn't able to enjoy it.

If you can't enjoy your success, what is the point of all the hard work?

The Magical Mystery Tour

Most human beings don't deliberately go off course and make themselves unhappy. However, what we sometimes fail to do is reflect, work out what's not working for us and then identify a plan of how we'd like to be as a person and what we'd like to move towards. Consequently, we end up on a magical mystery tour, being surprised by the crap that turns up along the way. We end up on a miserable mystery tour.

As a kid the thing I longed for the most was my mum and dad getting back together. I used to fantasise about this listening to Dad's signature music, which was Jean-Michel Jarre, (let's call him JMJ for short). Whenever we saw Pops, he'd play JMJ in his beige Ford Cortina. It was that rusty that when he drove over a puddle, he'd say, 'lift your feet up girls, you might get wet.' To be honest, the music sounded like squeaky bike wheels to me, but I loved it because it represented him. Listening to JMJ's album Oxygene on a cassette tape on my Sony Walkman whisked me off to that land of happy ever after.

Well, be careful what you wish for people! They did get back together in my teens. When it actually happened, it was a little strange. Anyway, as part of our family reunion trips together, my Dad asked us if we wanted to go and see JMJ at a 'free' concert in the London Docklands. I leapt at the chance, regardless of how uncool liking JMJ was for me at that stage in my life.

Off we set, all excited. Going to London on the train, eating sandwiches from the buffet car and drinking tea from Styrofoam cups felt like a real treat for us. We rarely ate out in those days and eating on a train counted as eating out!

When we arrive, I realise my Dad doesn't know the specific location of the concert or what time it starts. As it begins to get dark, we can see that the show is already in progress. When I ask where we are heading, he said, 'Let's follow the lights.' JMJ used to do a laser beam show synced to his music – it was innovative in the 80s, (sat here chuckling as I think about this now).

We wander through what seemed like endless meandering

dark terraced streets, with crowds of other people in search of the free concert. This was partly reassuring as it meant that we weren't the only fools on a directionless mission. I can't tell you how frustrated I felt. We were so near, yet so far and had no plan as to how to get to our destination; we didn't know where our destination was. Even now I still get irritated if my husband takes me on a *magical mystery tour* – I hate wasting time, (note to self, I probably need to Haven that). Anyway, we arrive at the concert as JMJ is saying 'au revoir'.

The magical mystery tour is something I see both in businesses and my one-to-one coaching work. We wonder how we end up at Destination Grim, getting results that we don't want and it's often because we don't take the time to:

- Recognise that we can be captains of our Ship and destiny by taking charge of the results we are getting in work-life.
- Reflect on what needs to change in our work-life.
- Align ourselves to the stars and own our gifts, talents and achievements.
- Get rid of the triggers that drown our joy, (more about this in Chapter 6).
- Identify our destination – a vision.
- Plan how we are going to achieve our vision, by identifying the goals and tasks that will get us there.

If we don't plan how to get to our vision, it's a fantasy.

Why Fantasising Screws up Your Navigation

Dr. Irena O'Brien, PhD a cognitive neuroscientist who has been studying psychology and neuroscience for over 20 years, draws on several studies in an article, which demonstrates that it is just fantasy if we simply visualise our outcomes, e.g. our vision of where we want to journey to. This is first because the brain struggles to differentiate between real and imagined. Secondly, studies have measured a drop in energy using systolic blood pressure.[27]

What this means is that if you're imagining the day when you've accomplished your outcome, your brain thinks you've already achieved it – so why bother mustering up energy and action to attain it!

Therefore, STOP fantasising or visualising what you will get at the end of your journey! You're decreasing your chances of reaching your goal / vision. What we need to do is programme our minds with the specific goals and tasks (the small steps) involved which will get us there NOT the destination. So, if you're going to fantasise, start visualising the small steps.

Natural, Unconscious Happiness and Success

It was no coincidence that Jennifer was happy with her lot and reached Destination Joy. She didn't fantasise about making changes, she took positive action – small steps in the right direction and came for regular coaching sessions to offload the Baggage that was causing drag. This resulted in Jennifer and her business being even more successful, without much effort.

When we remove what's dragging us down, we become more efficient and effective. We're no longer wasting brain calories and time on the things that have triggered us. We can breeze through work-life more easily. We build resilience so that when the waters get choppy and work-life throws us some waves, (because it will), we have enough buoyancy to ride the storm.

ACTION:

- When someone triggers you, e.g. upsets, hurts, annoys, disappoints etc. how many people do you discuss it with? How long does this take? What impact does it have on your focus?

- How much time do you spend ruminating when you are triggered? What is the impact of this? How does it affect you personally? Do you lose sleep? How does this influence your performance at work? What is the impact on your family and friends?

Jennifer got promoted to a different role which suited her talents, skills and abilities. She was able to comfortably tell clients that she couldn't see them for 6 weeks, (because she was good at what she did) as opposed to trying to squeeze everything onto her 'production line' (more on this in Chapter 7) and working herself into the ground. Her clients continued to queue up. She was able to enjoy family time again, be present and relax straight into holidays. The tension she held in her shoulders disappeared.

Destination Joy: Vision

Recently we went away with our friends to the Lake District. Ali and I went on a little horse-riding jaunt around the knobbly fells, whilst the rest of the gang watched the rugby. Afterwards, we met up in their apartment. With Prosecco in hand, I'm stood like John Wayne in my smelly jodhpurs, admiring the view of the marina. Then I realise we'd rented the apartment next door, 11 years ago.

Back then I was 5 months pregnant. I felt ecstatically happy. It had been a long road getting to this point. My bump now visible, called for expandable sweatpants. I'm sat on the floor feeling all goodie-two-shoes having completed my daily baby yoga DVD when it occurs to me that we need a vision board! Our lives were about to change.

My husband appears from the bedroom and has barely opened his eyes when I ask him what he would like from our future together as a new family. Again, he knew that look – overenthusiastic and too early in the morning. He said: 'Draw me a boat on Lake Windermere.' I thought, *a bit random, he's never mentioned an interest in boats before, but Ok, cool.*

Eight years later, we buy Lady Be, an 'Entry-level boat' we were reminded of by the salesman. Our caravan on water. And there we were, my friend and I clinking our Prosecco glasses looking out on the marina at Lady Be. Who'd have thought it ay?

Often vision and mission get confused when I work with organisations. Think of a vision as a Big Hairy Audacious Goal, (BHAG) a future destination you want to travel to; a term used in *Built to Last: Successful Habits of Visionary Companies.*[28] Something that you want to achieve or become. Earlier in Chapter 3, you considered your Position A, which is where you are right now. Your Position B is where you want to move towards – your vision.

A mission on the other hand is something that is a constant regardless of where you are journeying to and is about what you do and your reason for existence. Do you remember me talking about my purpose, which is expressed through my mission and strapline, 'optimising brilliance'? This has stayed with me the 14 years I have been in business and helps me to decide which projects I will and won't accept, regardless of what vision I have set myself. My current business vision statement is: *To make Beee a transferable business so that I can work anywhere in the UK.*

Because my work and life are so intertwined, (as are probably yours) this vision statement also guides my personal life. It is my private life which instigated my current vision. I would love to be able to move my family to either a mountainous location or somewhere near the sea once my husband retires so that he can do long dog walks and tend his garden. I also want to ensure that my daughter gets the educational start she needs in life by going to a great school so that she is embedded in a community that she loves and feels part of.

I would like to be able to coach, train and develop people and businesses any time, any place, anywhere, (not on roller skates, in a mini skirt with a bottle or Martini on a tray – although it could be fun, but might be off-putting for my clients).

I would like to work even more flexibly, so that I can spend quality stretches with my husband in his retirement, for example, conducting a coaching session via Zoom on the boat in the morning and then popping off for a sail in the afternoon. I'd like to be able to provide support to my girl as she needs it, through what can be turbulent years, as humans go from a teenager to an adult.

The aspects for me? The mountains, (this is connected to my past having lived in the Lakes when I was 12, for a year. It was the happiest time of my childhood). The sea, (I'm from Costa del Morecambe and am so used to seeing the sea – it makes me feel free). Both hills and water take my breath away. They put everything into perspective. They cleanse my soul. I love the beauty of nature, (this is connected to my values).

This vision is something that both my husband and I share along with some core values. We keep the vision alive by discussing it regularly. We move towards it by getting into the nitty-gritty of the plan. Writing this book is part of the plan! Hey, maybe I'll coach you one day via Zoom!

All of that from one measly line. Do you get where we're going with this? Can you see how things begin to link and connect?

So, we have already covered your purpose (or mission) in Chapter 4. Your next step is to identify your vision which should outline what you want to achieve as part of the process in this book. What are all the things that are going to make you shine? What's your version of Destination Joy? Typically, when I'm coaching individuals or organisations, we work on a 5 – 10 year vision. You're the captain of this voyage though, so you decide what timescale you would like.

Vision Statement Checklist

A vision statement should be:

- Easy to remember. It should create an anchor point which will help you to focus your mind and assess whether any future actions, decisions or behaviours take you closer to or further away from Destination Joy – your vision.
- 1 – 2 sentences and no more than 30 words.
- About what you want to become or achieve in the future.
- Stretching and a little scary, but not totally unrealistic. It's OK if you can't immediately see how you are going to get to Destination Joy, that's where your goals and tasks come in, which I will cover next.
- Inspiring and motivate you to act.
- Linked to your strengths, values and purpose.
- Meaningful to you. My vision statement is a bland sentence – but it's all the things it represents to *me*.

ACTION:

- As you begin to think about Destination Joy, what words spring to mind? Write them down in your *Inner Brilliance, Outer Shine Workbook*. Consider your:
  - Strengths
  - Values
  - Purpose
  - Snapshot. What do you want to change? What is the polar positive opposite of what is happening right now for you? What will it be like when your imposter syndrome has been silenced and your workaholic habits kicked to the curb?
- Next, highlight the 6 words from above that absolutely must be included in your vision statement.
- Now, create your vision statement using 1 – 2 sentences and no more than 30 words.

- Finally, go back to the Vision Statement Checklist earlier in this chapter and double-check it meets the criteria.
- Allow your vision statement to percolate. Put it on a sticky somewhere prominent and keep coming back to it. Tweak it. Refine it until you're happy with it.

Be the Brave Captain

The last few words about visions. Visions keep you alive, moving forward and relevant. They keep you enthusiastic about life because otherwise, we get stuck in the mundanity of it all. If we fail to fully explore what we are capable of – what a waste of talent! If we fail to really access the joy of work-life whilst we walk this planet – what a waste of time!

As I have previously mentioned, I like to think of us all being work in progress but in a growth mindset way, not in a 'you're never good enough' way. Having new territory to explore makes work-life exciting. You can do plenty of Havening work, (which you'll do in the next chapter and I have done *shiploads* of), but then if you do nothing with the beautiful being that is you and don't dare to try out new things to keep work-life interesting, you could run the risk of getting bored and blue. Be the Brave Captain. Go and set that stretch vision.

When clients are scared of their stretch vision, I talk to them about the swimming pool analogy. My daughter will happily spend most of her holiday in water. She gets frustrated with me because I do the whole, edge in bit by bit, allowing the water to slowly creep up to my waist. She will shout, 'Oh come onnnn mummy. Hurry up!' Then, before I know it, I'm fully submerged and off! It is the same with our visions. If we action one task after another (more about these later), before we know it, we are waist-deep in our vision and half-way towards achieving it. The fear has dissipated, and the destination is in sight.

Ports of Call: Goals

To reach your desired destination, you are going to need a plan, otherwise, we are at risk of failing to arrive at Destination Joy. You wouldn't dream of chartering a boat around the world without working out your ports of call. It would be too big a distance to cover. It's the same with your vision. We need to break it down into manageable chunks, the first of which will be your goals – what you need to achieve to attain your vision. Followed by how you are going to achieve your goals – your tasks.

Four Types of Goal

In Science Daily, they quote a study by the Department of Psychology at the University of Wyoming in which they analysed the language used in goals. There are four categories of goal.

1. Prominence, which covers goals ranging from power and moneymaking to perfection and glory, but most strongly reflects the pursuit of social status – the desire to earn the respect, admiration and deference of others through one's achievements.
2. Inclusiveness, which covers a goal to open-mindedly accept people of all types.
3. Negativity prevention, which covers goals to avoid a wide variety of negative outcomes, including conflict, disagreement, isolation and social discord.
4. Tradition, which includes a desire to uphold the long-standing institutions of one's culture – including religion, family, nation and other group values.[29]

When I read this research and reflected on my current goals, it made sense and I could fit them into the above categories. Now, please don't mould your goals to fit this research. I share this research with you to reassure you. You are normal. Other people are doing this stuff.

As you think about the voyage you are going to embark on as you read this book, what do you need to do to reach your vision? Ensure that whatever goals you set, everything is aligned with your:

- Snapshot(s) – what you want to change.
- Strengths – what you're good at. We can end up at Destination Grim if we pursue a dream that doesn't suit our skills and abilities.
- Values – I advise caution here. You can go completely off course if you fail to factor in what's important to you. For example, if in our next house move, we forget to include our value of privacy, we would be miserable.
- Purpose – how you make a difference in this world. For years I banged on about having a café. Yes, I could potentially optimise brilliance with the staff I employed, but I wouldn't be helping nearly enough people to shine!

ACTION:

- What are the main subject areas (think in big chunks which involve multiple tasks) that could contribute towards achieving your vision? For example, to attain my current vision, the topics involved include:

  - Home location
  - Marketing
  - Products (this book)
  - Finance

Call me old fashioned, but SMART goals still serve my clients and me well. Although I do tend to drop the 'A' which stands for 'Achievable', as I believe in shooting for the moon. Questioning whether something is achievable can cause self-doubt and we can begin to talk ourselves out of the thing that we are trying to achieve. So, it is more like SMRT.

Also, according to Christopher Bergland world-class endurance athlete, coach and author of *The Athlete's Way: Sweat and the Biology of Bliss*, we can make ourselves happier and increase the confidence molecule serotonin, by challenging ourselves regularly and going after things that reinforce a sense of purpose, meaning, and accomplishment.[30] We're back to being a Brave Captain again.

I've seen a variety of different meanings for SMRT objectives, but this is the one that I think is the best:

- S – Specific: What specifically do you want to achieve?
- M – Measurable: How will you know when you have attained the goal? What evidence will you have?
- R – Relevant: How is this goal connected to your Vison? Why are you doing this?
- T – Time-bound: When will you have attained the goal?

The next step is to turn these subject areas into goals and write them down. If you're hesitating and thinking about skipping this step, in a study by psychologist Gail Matthews, she identified that people were 33% more successful in achieving their desired outcomes when they wrote their goals down, as opposed to keeping them in their head.[31]

ACTION:

- Write up to four goals (any more could dilute your focus) which will deliver your vision using SMRT. Each goal should define what you want to achieve, not how you will achieve it, e.g. To have completed the first draft of my book by 2019. The 'how' will be covered next.

Plotting the Course: Tasks

When you begin plotting a course as a sailor, there are two important things you need to know: where you are currently at, (your Snapshot) and where you want to travel to, (your Vision). You must know where you are, at any time by spotting the navigation aids such as buoys and lighthouses. These will help you to know whether you are on or off course. Your tasks will become your navigation aids guiding you through your ports of call (your goals) to your destination (your vision) and make the voyage less scary.

Part of what makes your vision and goals scary is that the chunks are too big. I procrastinated over writing this book for 10 years. I hadn't plotted my course. I hadn't broken down the goal into micro-steps – tasks. Also, I had limiting beliefs that were creating drag on the project, such as, *I haven't got enough time. I don't know how to write a book,* (even though I'd read several books on the topic and attended a book writing course).

I'd started and stopped writing my book countless times. Then one day, I met with a client for lunch. We strayed into personal topics and I somehow got on the subject of my book. I had been keeping her held to account through coaching for the last 6 months, and here I was confessing that I'd not achieved one of my aspirations. I made more excuses as she probed further. I defended my lack of action. I cringed as I walked away. I made myself a promise to do better next time.

I had to identify all the small steps (tasks) involved in achieving my goal. The first task was to email a book coach and find out how they could help. Not scary. Not having to write anything yet. The initial person I spoke to laughed when I said how long I'd been writing my book. I didn't take that relationship forward. I felt stupid, got scared again and so I procrastinated some more.

Then, as I was running a course and encouraging the delegates to set goals for the programme I asked them to agree to take, *One small step within the next 24 hours which would get them off the starting blocks and moving towards their goal.* I'd managed to prick my conscience. I needed to be the Brave Captain.

Coincidently, another book coach called Debbie Jenkins connected with me whilst the delegates were on a break. Very serendipitous. I dropped her an email to say that it could be worth us talking. This was the second task. We booked a Zoom call, (third task) and when we spoke, the chemistry was right this time. I felt so inspired and excited. I signed up to her coaching programme (fourth task). Book writing no longer felt scary. We worked out a plan together, (fifth task). I was going to reserve every Monday in my diary to write, (sixth task). Small steps add up to the achievement of a big goal.

Incidentally, in the goal setting study I mentioned earlier, those people that had to report on their goals weekly, achieved significantly more than all other groups. Working with my coach helped me to be accountable and stay on track. I made promises to her after each session, then we would review those tasks when we met next. It only worked!

ACTION:

- Tasks identify how you will achieve a goal. List all the tasks involved in each goal for the next 12 months. Work out what you need to do and when you need to do it by.

Programming the Quickest Route into Your Ship's Navigation System

The brain processes a picture 60,000 times quicker than a word. In a study conducted by a team of neuroscientists from MIT (Massachusetts Institute of Technology) they discovered that the brain can process entire images that the eye sees for as little as 13 milliseconds.[32] To put this into context, it takes you 300 to 400 milliseconds to blink your eye, which is 1/3 of a second. This means that your brain can identify what it's looking at, approximately 30 times faster than you can blink your eye.

So, to apply the science, and efficiently programme our brains with the goals and tasks we want to achieve that will take us to our Destination Joy, we need to draw!

When I first set up Beee, I used to run an intensive 13-day course called The Enabling Excellence Programme. As part of this programme, delegates became NLP Practitioners but also spent a day envisioning their future. I would get the audience to discuss, write and then draw their vision, goals and tasks on a large piece of paper. Drawing can often make delegates feel uneasy because many people haven't picked up a set of crayons since they were at school.

In the spirit of sharing that vulnerability, I would show them a picture I had drawn for my vision and goals. The picture included a three-storey, Georgian house, which was big enough for me to see my clients at home. At the time looking at this picture seemed like an unachievable pipedream. Then several years later having settled into our new home I came across my old vision and goals board. Our house was almost a replica of the one I'd drawn.

ACTION:

Your final activity for this chapter is to commit crayon, coloured pencils, felt tips or paint to paper. The more colourful the better. Using your goals and tasks as a guide, draw all the things involved in moving you towards your Destination Joy – your vision.

Then, put it somewhere prominent where you can review it regularly. My current drawing sits in my in-tray, which includes scribbles relating to writing this book!

Summary of Key Points:

To avoid Destination Grim and the miserable mystery tour:

- Identify your Destination Joy – your vision. Write it down in less than 30 words and no more than 2 sentences.
- Then work out your ports of call – your goals. What do you need to achieve to reach your vision?
- Plot your course – avoid going adrift by working out all the tasks involved in delivering each goal. This is the 'how' of your goal.
- Be the Brave Captain and shoot for the moon. You can make yourself happier and more confident by stretching yourself and accomplishing new things linked to your purpose.
- Avoid visualising the destination you want to head towards; studies show that you will screw up your navigation system. Stop damaging your motivation by fooling your brain into believing you've already accomplished your dream. You will increase your chances of success if you write down how you are going to achieve your vision through your goals and tasks. You can cement these choices and appeal to both sides of your brain by also drawing what it is that you are going to do.

Chapter 6

Antidote #6: Offload Excess Baggage

A ship in harbour is safe, but that is not what ships are built for.
J. A. Shedd

An overloaded boat is more likely to capsize, particularly in bad weather or choppy waters. A boat floats because its density is less than the density of the water. However, if there is too much cargo on board its mass becomes greater than the water, and it sinks.

Sometimes we can feel weighed down by the Baggage of our work-life. We may even consider abandoning ship, because work-life is too much, and we are at risk of sinking. I see it regularly in my coaching practice, particularly those with imposter syndrome and workaholic habits. Take Vanessa, she was working all hours for a very difficult client. A real perfectionist and a black and white thinker. If events and conversations weren't as expected at work, she struggled to see things from a different perspective; to think flexibly. Her fixed mindset was weighing her down. She was so conscientious; an all-round good egg and yet failed to get the recognition she craved from her employer. This was because she had a reputation for being gloomy, which took the shine off all her other great qualities.

At the end of her coaching programme, she was rewarded with her coveted pay rise and promotion. As she got up to leave my office, she paused by the door and said, 'Thank you so much for your help. I'm not sure I would still be here; had I not been coached.' She had been contemplating abandoning her Ship.

Before a storm, ships seek a safe harbour. In this chapter, you're going to discover your port in a storm. Whilst you are in the safety of your port, you are going to offload any Baggage which is causing drag on your Ship. You know the stuff that slows you down and makes you ineffective and inefficient? The stuff that triggers emotional waves and prevents you from presenting your best shiny self. The stuff that creates those inner imposter thoughts and causes you to overwork. The stuff that stops you from experiencing the joy of your work-life.

You're going to equip yourself with a tool which I refer to as my 'Silver Bullet'. When I qualified as a coach I got frustrated quite early on in my career. I couldn't understand why some clients would spend two hours discussing a problem and identifying actions and solutions, only to return the following session and not changed a thing. I realised that sometimes inner stuff got in the way of the outer behaviours that would make their work-life better.

In my quest to continue to make a difference, I went in search of other tools which would help my clients to make the changes they wanted to make. I became an NLP Practitioner, Master Practitioner and then Trainer. I studied hypnotherapy and Integral Eye Movement Therapy. I learnt how to use EFT (Emotional Freedom Technique) – this is good and I will show you how to use it in Chapter 9. Then I found Havening.

With Havening, my clients didn't have to believe in it, it simply worked. They could be as sceptical as they liked. As long as they'd accessed a memory and they were carrying out the Havening touch, it changed the way the memory was encoded and got rid of the feeling which triggered the unhelpful behaviour. Havening is my go-to tool. Ninety per cent of all my coaching clients use Havening. It's simply amazeballs. Not only has it dramatically changed my own life it continues to change the life of my clients. It's so simple, quick and easy to use that my daughter Havened her friend when she was 7 years old. She had fallen over and hurt her knee and was very upset, so my daughter used Havening to calm her down. To an onlooker, it would have seemed like she was providing reassuring support.

Recently there was a car crash at the end of our street. The driver that caused the accident was hysterical and close to panic. A passing nurse stopped to help. With good intentions, she said, 'Oh dear, are you panicking?' This seemed to escalate the symptoms and the driver's breathing became more erratic and she said she felt faint and sick. In Chapter 8 I will explain how words influence minds.

I'd been reading a book called *The Worst Is Over: What To Say When Every Moment Counts*[33], and had learnt that we can help people to heal quicker following an accident, by using words more effectively, such as, 'The worst is over now. Help is on its way. You are safe.' I repeated these words and explained that I could use Havening to help her to feel calmer. She agreed and within moments her breathing began to return to normal, she stopped crying and shouting. She was able to think more clearly as she spoke to the Police Officer. So quick and simple, so let's get on and start lightening the load of your ship.

Are You Exceeding Your Baggage Allowance?

In a study of 9,508 people, conducted by the Department of Preventive Medicine, Southern California Permanente Medical Group (Kaiser Permanente), San Diego 92111, USA, they analysed the impact of Adverse Childhood Experiences, (ACE) and found 'a strong graded relationship between the breadth of exposure to abuse or household dysfunction during childhood and multiple risk factors for several of the leading causes of death in adults.'[34] More specifically, they looked at those childhood experiences which occurred between the ages of 0-7 – we're back to Chapter 3 again and the imprint period! There are 10 types of childhood trauma, which gives you an ACE score. The more traumas or points we score, the higher the risk of health conditions as an adult. Here are the categories of adverse childhood experiences:

Numbers 1 – 5 relate to things that happen to you personally.

Numbers 6 – 10 are about other family members:

1. Physical abuse
2. Verbal abuse
3. Sexual abuse
4. Physical neglect
5. Emotional neglect
6. A parent who's an alcoholic
7. A mother who's a victim of domestic violence
8. A family member in jail
9. A family member diagnosed with a mental illness
10. The disappearance of a parent through divorce, death or abandonment.

Each category of trauma counts as one point. So, for example, if a person was hit by a parent (1), regularly belittled (1), observed their mother being beaten up (1), had a father who used drugs and got drunk (1), which resulted in their mother suffering depression (1), and the child being ignored and feeling unloved (1), then ultimately the parent leaving (1), the ACE score soon tots up.

I appreciate this all sounds very depressing. The good news is that you can use Havening like a magic eraser to get rid of any traumatic memories, thereby potentially decreasing your ACE score.

ACTION:

- Work out your ACE score. Use the Crow's Nest position to avoid taking a deep dive into any difficult Baggage until you get to the Havening protocol.
- When you get to the section of this chapter which is about finding unwanted Baggage, the memories relating to your ACE score could be a good place to start.

In Chapter 3 I spoke about big and little traumas. The big traumas are those listed above. Equally, we can have lots of little traumas weighing us down, such as children calling us names in the playground at school or not being able to tie our shoelaces. The point is that it all depends on the meaning we attach to these events. If having struggled to tie our shoelaces following a P.E. lesson, we mistakenly interpreted this event to mean that we're not as good as our peers – that needs to be erased.

Sometimes we have outdated programmes that no longer serve us. Consider Havening a software update to get rid of the glitches in your navigation system. You wouldn't dream of not updating an app on a device or your PC, (I accept you might delay it) especially if it wasn't working properly. Remember, this is *project me time*. Once your programmes have been updated, you'll find that you get to where you need to go, much quicker, with less effort and more shine.

More Shine

What do I mean by more shine? I'll paint a picture of what no shine looks like first.

I was running a series of personal effectiveness training sessions. It was the first module and I'd got a group of positive, trendy and upbeat people; that was until the last member of the team arrived. She was late. Instantly the atmosphere changed. The delegates quietened. The lady burst in with her head down; there was no eye contact with anyone. She noisily unpacked her laptop and began typing straight away like she was sending some urgent Morse Code message. One of her colleagues asked her if she wanted a herbal tea.

Her hair was greasy and lank, and she had the familiar stress spots, (takes one to know one). She was so pale. I was concerned about her. At the break, I took her to one side and asked if everything was OK. She looked unwell. She said that she had been working on a very important assignment through the night and that the deal wasn't done yet. She would need to work on the contract whilst she was on the course. I asked her if she wanted to leave but she insisted on staying put.

She was a workaholic. I could see the potential genius within. However, it was tarnished with whatever was going on for her. She managed to busily tap away on her computer, take phone calls and prepare and deliver a presentation on the same day. She wasn't shining though. She was half doing things. Busy multitasking, but also having a negative impact on the team around her. She had the potential to be so much more. She was lacking in joy.

When I do deep change work with clients, i.e. use a technique to clear up past stuff, one of the benefits can be that they physically look better. I saw my client Danielle recently on a team day following one to one work and I couldn't help staring at her. She looked somehow taller and younger. Her complexion looked creamier and smoother, (she'd not had Botox before you wonder). She had so much more energy.

As we caught up Danielle spoke about experiencing peace and tranquillity for the first time in her life. She had space for joy because her body was no longer swamped by stress and pain. Whilst I don't specialise in clearing health conditions for clients, that can be one of the inadvertent benefits. Heal the emotion. Dissipate the emotional pain.

When she started working with me she had chronic back pain. If she got an attack, she would have to clear her diary and would sleep on the floor for days. She described it as an 'inconvenience for everyone' because it had such a broad impact on her family, friends and employer.

Danielle was shining because she'd cleared lots of past childhood events using Havening. It was also down to her taking charge of her life. She was managing her boundaries (more about this in Chapter 7) and no longer accepting unacceptable behaviour. She got promoted to a new role within the business which suited her talents and abilities. She learnt to acknowledge what she was thinking and feeling.

Before coaching Danielle would over-empathise with others and happily resolve their problems, whilst numbing and rejecting her thoughts and feelings. She was another good egg! All that suppressing resulted in back pain, but once she began acknowledging what was going on and made herself a priority, it disappeared. She learnt to take care of herself first, before taking care of others. She realised that when she didn't do that, she was no good to anyone. She'd redirected herself to Destination Joy.

When we offload Baggage and tensions within, our muscles relax. When we let go of negativity, joy and peace can make an appearance. This in turn enables us to shine more.

What is Havening?

Havening is a derivative of the word haven, which can also mean a place of safety, a port, dock or harbour. Havening is a method which is designed to change the brain to de-traumatize the memory and remove its negative effects from both our psyche and body. These techniques have been developed and refined since 2001. The first official training occurred in May 2013 in the UK.

Havening is a psychosensory technique which uses sensory input to alter thought, mood and behaviour. Havening involves touch, (more about this later) and can be self-applied, unlike a lot of therapies. This is great news as it puts you back in charge as the Captain.

What can Havening be Used for?

You can use Havening for a variety of things including:

- Altering limiting beliefs impacting on confidence, self-

esteem and ultimately work performance
- Releasing general negative feelings, e.g. a need to control
- Embedding positive messages
- Reducing unhelpful emotions/states such as:
  - Stress
  - Anger
  - Anxiety
  - Guilt
  - Shame and embarrassment
  - Jealousy
  - Fear
- Removing unnecessary ideas about aspects of the future
- Dealing with performance anxiety, e.g. Presenting
- Treating emotional responses resulting from past negative events
- Eliminating phobias
- Reducing chronic pain (when a psychological component underlies)
- Eradicating recurring nightmares / night terrors
- Dealing with grief
- Post-Traumatic Stress Disorder, (PTSD)
- Emotional eating

At the time of writing this book Havening does not help with:

- Addictive and obsessive/compulsive behaviours
- Certain pain syndromes and vasovagal (e.g. fainting)

How Havening was Created
The Havening Techniques have been developed by Ronald A. Ruden M.D., Ph.D. along with his brother Steven J. Ruden, D.D.S., ICF/ACCDr.

Ronald is a doctor who runs a private medical practice in Manhattan. He has a PhD in neuropharmacology, which is a branch of neuroscience involving the study of drugs that alter the nervous system and its functioning, specifically within the brain. Dr. Ron as he is affectionately known is an authentic, kind, gentle genius with a genuine interest in making people's lives better.

Steven is a Doctor of Dental Surgery and a certified hypnotherapist. He is also a consultant and coach for individuals and Fortune 500 companies. Stephen has collaborated with his twin brother for over 10 years in the development of the Havening Techniques. He too is passionate about the eradication of trauma and has published in the area of dental phobias.

Ronald came across TFT, (Thought Field Therapy) created by Roger Callahan, PhD and was interested in the results it was producing. For example, a woman with a longstanding phobia of water was able to jump into a swimming pool and splash her face, having tapped certain points of her body. Unfortunately, there was no science supporting this technique, so Dr. Ron spent 7 years investigating the various psychosensory techniques which were out there, to establish which ones produced changes in the brain. In doing so, he was able to design an optimised set of protocols known as The Havening Techniques®.

Originally designed to help treat people with PTSD (Post Traumatic Stress Disorder), Havening can be used to deal with traumatic or stressful memories. For the purposes of this book, and for the majority of my clients, we use Havening to clear up the events from their past, often in their childhood, which are limiting their success and preventing them from presenting the best version of themselves in their work-lives.

How Does Havening Work?

When we think about negative events, whether real or imagined, (as the brain doesn't distinguish between the two, so someone could be vicariously traumatised by hearing a description of 9/11), as we recall the event, the neural pathway where the memory is encoded is live for 7 minutes. This means the receptors on the postsynaptic neuron will be protracted and cause us to re-experience the feelings. Hence why throughout this book I have been encouraging you to use the Crow's Nest so that you don't fully access the memories you want to change and begin re-feeling. However, you can consciously choose to do so, once you know how to use Havening to get rid of them.

Ron discovered that by stimulating the skin on your face, arms and the palms of your hands we produce serotonin and delta waves. This then triggers calcineurin which causes the receptors to retract. The result is that (if correctly applied) you can't reproduce the limiting feeling(s).

In Chapter 3 I shared that I used to be claustrophobic and had a fear of heights. This was inconvenient. It meant that I couldn't get into lifts. On my 30th birthday, my husband took me to New York. As a 'treat' we went to the Empire State Building. I took one look at the lift and ran off. I was so frustrated with myself and my poor husband had to go up on his own.

Compare this with a recent ski trip where I had to go in a gondola to get up the mountain; I didn't bat an eyelid. I forgot that I used to have these fears. I couldn't reproduce the feelings or the over-thinking. It was only when I was in the 'high up lift' on my own recording a vlog that I remembered. You can watch the vlog here on my YouTube channel:

https://www.youtube.com/watch?v=aJLTnWi2bww.

It Might Feel Like Magic

In Chapter 9 I will be talking about how we can influence our state of mind in more detail, but for now, if we work on the premise that our feelings, drive our behaviour, we can, therefore, change how we behave, by changing our feelings. This is where Havening seems like magic. Once we change the feelings associated with the present-day trigger, when we go back into that context, we don't have to think about behaving differently, it simply occurs. This is because the trigger has been removed.

I've heard the most sceptical clients talk about their change following Havening. I once coached an executive called Heather, who preferred to work with me on more clinical matters like strategy and business development. She didn't believe in discussing feelings. However, she wasn't getting the results she wanted whilst out networking. In our session, she confessed that when she stood up to do her elevator pitch, she would get an involuntary cough, which made her feel like she shouldn't be speaking. This was a lady who had a big personality and was well known in the business community.

As I listened, I asked her the magic question, 'When in the distant past, (ideally age 0-7) have you felt that you shouldn't have been speaking?' Heather said, 'Infront of my childless aunt who said, "Children should be seen and not heard in adult company".' Whenever Heather was in a group setting with other adults, she was re-triggered into feeling like she shouldn't be talking.

After the session, she dusted herself off and said, 'Thank you very much. That was strange and I don't think anything has changed.'

The following morning, I got a call. Heather had been networking. She was ringing to let me know that she'd just stood up and was able to do her elevator pitch without coughing. Her words flowed out eloquently. She achieved that without any preparation or effort on her part. Havening the memory of her aunt saying what she said, changed the limiting belief, behaviour and feelings. As Paul Daniels used to say, 'Now, that's what I call magic.'

Does Havening Really Work?

In my coaching practice, Havening is the technique I use the most. What fascinates me is that I can be part-way through

Havening an event and when the client returns the following month or sometimes even years later and we pick up where they left off, nine times out of ten, the client will score the memory as they did in their last session. Whilst this isn't scientific proof of the permanence of Havening work, it is great anecdotal evidence.

If an issue isn't resolved it's usually because the root cause memory hasn't been worked on. More about this later.

If you're still feeling sceptical about Havening, I get it. You've almost got to experience it to believe it. In a recent study to prove Havening's efficacy, the Academic Department of Military Mental Health at King's College London, identified that a single session of Havening had a positive impact on probable depression, probable anxiety and work and social adjustment. The participants were reported as being occupationally impaired.[35]

What to Expect from Havening

In all honesty, you will have your own unique experience, but I can tell you about some of the repeated anecdotes from my clients. They report feeling:

- Relaxed, often sleepy whilst using the Havening touch. This is because of the delta waves, which we usually experience during sleep.
- Lighter and de-stressed as if a load has been taken off their shoulders.
- As though the traumatic event is more of a fact, without any emotional content. This is because the receptors which created the emotions have retracted; they've been depotentiated.
- Balanced, calmer, less nagging inner dialogue and more like themselves – as though the reset button has been pressed.

- That their behaviour simply changes without any conscious effort because they're no longer being triggered emotionally. Often their realisations of change only occur when they re-wind the tape or I check in with them to ensure the issue has been resolved. They seem to have lots of, 'Oh yes. I forgot that was ever an issue' moments.

- Finally, one of my observations, is that their limiting belief language changes. This is real unconscious stuff that is often out of their conscious awareness and their look of surprise when we review their original warts and all Snapshot of how things were, is priceless. Some can't believe they said the things they said.

The Small Print

Although Havening appears to have promising emotional, mental, and physical health benefits, Havening has yet to be fully researched by the Western academic, medical, and psychological communities. Therefore, Havening may be considered experimental, and the extent of its effectiveness, as well as its risks and benefits, are not fully known. Havening is self-regulated and is considered alternative or complementary to the healing arts that are licensed in the United States.[36]

Please do not use the Havening Technique with yourself for serious trauma or if you suffer from any psychological disorders. We advise that you seek the help of a professional mental health care provider who is certified in the Havening Technique if you have experienced severe trauma or suffer from a psychological disorder.[37]

Additionally, because the memory will likely change in terms of how it is encoded in your brain, I would advise against Havening anything which you might be required to present evidence on in court, as the way you recall it will more than likely be different.

Finally, please stay safe and don't operate machinery whilst carrying out the Havening touch and ensure that you feel sufficiently alert following treatment, for example, to drive.

So now it's your turn to make a port of call to your safe haven.

Part 1: Understand the Havening Procedure

I'm going to share the protocol for Havening first before you start exploring which memories you want to Haven so that you are familiar with the process and can start as soon as you identify a memory. The Havening procedure is beautifully simple.

1. **Think about the memory momentarily.** If you get full-on, intense feelings, go straight to step 3 and begin the Havening touch.
2. **If the event doesn't seem to trigger any feelings,** which can be the case for smaller traumas, it can be useful to identify the submodalities. These are the detail of how a memory is encoded through our modalities (our senses). Identifying the detail can help you fully access the event. When you Haven a memory, you may notice that some elements of it change, e.g. what you see as you recall it may change from being in colour to black and white. As you think about the memory, ask yourself these questions:

- Is the memory in colour or black and white?
- Is it a movie or a still picture?
- Can you see yourself in it or are you looking out of your own eyes?
- Is it easy to see or fuzzy?
- Is there anything you can hear?
- Where can you hear the sound? Is it in your left or right ear or is it surround sound?
- What's the volume of the sound like? High, medium or low?

- Is the sound continuous or discontinuous?
- What was the younger you feeling back then?
- Where do you get that feeling?
- Does the feeling have a shape, colour, temperature or texture?
- Is the feeling static or does it move?
- Finally, are there any tastes or smells present?

3. **Score the level of negativity on a scale of 0 – 10**, 10 being the strongest negative feeling, 0 meaning all feeling has gone. Trust the first number that pops into your head as this will be your true unconscious score.

4. **Begin the Havening touch**. You can repeatedly sweep your hands:
- Over your face,
- Down from your shoulders to your elbows,
- Or rub the palms of your hands together - whichever is most comfortable using a stroking speed which suits you.

5. **Now distract yourself with something pleasant** e.g. counting footsteps in the sand or simply watching an uplifting or positive TV programme. When I'm working with my clients, depending on the intensity of feelings being experienced, we explore solutions to their coaching topics as a form of distraction.

6. **Continue the Havening touch for 7 minutes**. I set a timer on my phone or use Alexa.

7. **Repeat** steps 1 – 6 above until the score is at zero.

You can find my 2-minute video on how to Self-Haven here: https://youtu.be/Mr8TkgIUxYI

Part 2: Find Unwanted Baggage

One of the things I love about Havening is that it seems to work with laser precision, whereas other techniques can be hit and miss. However, Havening relies on you being able to identify the source memory. For example, if you wanted to get rid of a dandelion in your garden, it would be no good simply pulling the stem and the leaves off the plant; you would need to treat the root to eradicate the weed for good and prevent it from growing back. You need to do the same with your memories and go to the root cause. To do this, you're going to become a Lost Baggage Detective.

Of course, you can Haven any recent adult events – particularly if this is a new trauma or upset. When I show groups how to self-haven, I get them to use it on a recent incident at work, e.g. not getting as much bonus as a colleague, which made you feel *unfairly treated*. However, if what you are experiencing is a recurring pattern in your life, i.e. feeling unfairly treated, that's a clue that there could be connections in your childhood. So, if you wanted to prevent this pattern coming back, you would need to find out where it comes from, e.g. at Christmas when you were 5 you felt unfairly treated compared to your siblings because they got more presents.

Another clue which could be an indication of childhood connections is how long the emotion persists. There is a difference between experiencing momentary anger for example if a cyclist drives you off a footpath, which dissipates almost as soon as their Lycra-clad legs disappear around the corner. Contrasted with the repeated uprising of anger each time you ruminate about the incident, which then wakes you in the middle of the night. These are clues.

Perhaps you catch yourself telling the tale of what happened to anyone that will listen; moaning and getting stuck in your story. We're back to playing victim or persecutor, which can also be signs that you have been re-triggered by 'old stuff'.

Therefore, to rid yourself of the limiting belief, behaviour or feeling you need to go back to the root cause, which should be your earliest childhood memory in the imprint period, age 0-7. Failing that, go to the earliest traumatic memory.

One final clue which can be an indication of an echo from the past at play is the presence of childlike phrases, such as:

- It's not fair.
- It's my fault.
- I did something wrong.
- Nobody likes me.
- I'm not good enough.
- I'm scared.
- I feel bad.

So, to summarise, to become a Lost Baggage Detective, you'll find clues by spotting:

- Recurring patterns of behaviour
- Emotions that persist long after the event has passed
- Child-like language

Part 3: Offload Excess Baggage

ACTION:

- Using a highlighter, review *The Inner Brilliance, Outer Shine Journal* and Snapshot to identify any clues in your language.
- Once you've spotted a clue, ask yourself this question:
  - What is my earliest memory, ideally age 0-7 of experiencing, [insert behaviour, emotion or language / belief]?
- Once you've found a memory, start the Havening protocol: in Part 1.

If you are not overloaded with feelings, you can simultaneously Haven many events together. Some of my clients have Havened up to 15 memories at once. This makes Havening an efficient method of change.

Good luck my friend. Let the magic begin! Go and take time for yourself to do this now. It could change your work-life.

Summary of Key Points:
- To offload excess Baggage so that your shine isn't tarnished, identify the events in your childhood, ideally age 0-7, which are connected to your present-day triggers. Then Haven them away.
- Havening should not be used if you need to retain certain aspects of the memory, for example, if you were to be a witness in court.
- Self-havening should not be administered for serious traumatic events. You can find a local Havening practitioner here: https://havening.org Alternatively, I work with clients via Zoom. Please get in touch at: estelle@beee.company.
- If you suffer from a psychological disorder, please seek out a mental health professional who is certified in The Havening Techniques.
- Finally, if you're questioning whether Havening works, start by using it on one memory – use it on something negative but low key and recent. If you're questioning whether you can be bothered, consider how much mental energy you use when you are triggered negatively and the results this gets you. What is the impact on your sleep, mental health, physical health, self-esteem, personal effectiveness, success, happiness, and joy? Remember it's *project me time*. Haven whilst you watch something positive on TV, which will serve as a distraction.

Chapter 7

Antidote #7: Run a Tight Ship

People treat you how you let them.
Mel Robbins

One of the things I have learnt personally but also from the client group I am writing this book for is that we must *run a tight ship* if we are going to keep our heads above water. For this chapter, it means being strict and disciplined with ourselves for our benefit, so that we're not overworking. This will go against the grain, but ultimately, it will be for everyone else's benefit too. We'll be much calmer, resourceful, resilient, happier and more effective creatures, to be with.

I've spoken about this group of people being good eggs. They put others first, generously give their time away, adding to-do's to their production line, at the risk of their health and wellbeing – not to mention the squeeze they put on their personal life. In this chapter, we are going to look at how to deal with any time and space stealers, which involves boundary management.

I'm probably going to encourage you to do things that will feel uncomfortable at first...but that's the thing with habits – change can be challenging. However, it will be worth it and you can use tools such as Havening and EFT (Emotional Freedom Technique – more about this in Chapter 9) to clear up any nurture based unconscious, automatic programmes which are preventing the change you want to achieve. What you stand to gain is to:

- Rid yourself of unnecessary tasks.
- Be able to spend your time on the things that are important to you, because time is the only commodity

we have. Did we have a good or bad time whilst we walked this planet?

- Consciously own your space and give off alternative vibes, so that you're not taken advantage of or burdened.
- Drive success by being able to focus on the results that you want.
- Create time and space so that you can access the joy of work-life.

Parkinson's Law

Cyril Northcote Parkinson was a British naval historian and author of 60 books. One of his most famous sayings was that 'Work expands so as to fill the time available for its completion'. So in other words, work will fill whatever time we give to it. There will always be stuff to be done and things on our to-do list, but if we don't allow space for not working, we end up working all the time!

One of my sayings is, 'We have to live life in the space in-between'. We must learn to stop the production line and go and enjoy ourselves. More on this in Chapter 10.

To apply Parkinson's Law, we have to have work-free time zones and manage our boundaries. I work from home and soon learnt to my detriment that I could work at any time. The office door would open easily and before I knew it, I'd be sucked down a rabbit hole and have lost half a day.

Time Boundaries

Work-free time zones are so important for workaholics. Learning to keep the door shut was one of the boundaries I had to set in place for myself. Door shut meant that it was time for personal time. Most of my clients know that if they want to get hold of me at the weekend or in the evenings, 1) it needs to be an emergency and 2) the best way to contact me is to send a text, as I rarely check in on my emails.

These basic rules mean that I can fully enjoy my time off with my family, rest, recharge and have fun, but also then do my best work when I'm with my clients. More about fun in chapter 10.

ACTION:

- What hours do you work currently? Don't give me your standard contractual hours. Think about it deeply. If you're unsure, raise awareness of when you are working over the next week.
- What hours would you like to work?
- What time boundaries could you set yourself, e.g. leave the office by 5 pm, don't look at emails after 7 pm, etc?
- What do you need to do to support this change? For example, store your work phone in the boot of your car and use autoresponder properly whilst on holiday or engaged, (none of this, 'I have limited access to my emails...' blah blah blah). This is a clue that a work time boundary may need strengthening. Either you're available or not right? Ease the pressure to check.

We've Got 4 Hours

Still not convinced that you should cut back your hours and have work-free time zones? According to Stanford's Alex Pang, author of *Rest: Why You Get More Done When You Work Less*, a knowledge worker should only work 4 hours.[38] Apparently, we can only concentrate and be involved in creative – real thinking activities for 4 hours. Beyond that our brain performs below par. Working longer hours becomes a false sense of economy. The likes of Charles Darwin knew this instinctively. He would work for two, 90-minute periods in the morning and then an hour later. So, if we only have 4 hours, what do we do with the rest of our time at work? We do tasks that we can perform on Autopilot. Yes, you get permission to switch your Autopilot on! Use this time to do the mind-numbing activities such as sifting through email, filing and admin. Give your brain a rest.

I work with lots of execs that run meetings back to back all day, without a break. It is no surprise they are knackered and not as effective as they could be. How can they possibly follow up on actions from a meeting? It is no wonder the to-do's start to stack up and the joy of their job has deserted them.

ACTION:
- How could you restructure your working week, so that you limit yourself to 4 hours thinking time a day?
- How could you pace your production line applying the 4-hour rule, e.g. I see clients for 2 hours in the morning and 2 hours in the afternoon, 2.5 days a week?

Your Production Line
Having worked for many manufacturing businesses, I use a production line analogy when talking to my clients about their workload:

- **Inputs at the start.** These are the tasks you put on your production line which you agree to do either consciously or *unconsciously*. How often is it assumed that you will do something and so you do!
- **Process in the middle.** This is you doing the work.
- **Outputs at the end.** This is task completion.

When we agree to do too much, tasks begin to build up. We get pressure from our 'customers' enquiring when their 'order' is going to be fulfilled. This adds more pressure. In this scenario, we have several strategies. We can:

- **Speed up the conveyor belt**, but then mistakes happen, and quality starts to be affected.
- **Extend productivity hours** and do overtime, but as we've

learnt that's a false sense of economy because we are not as effective if we break the 4-hour thinking rule.

- **Keep the production line going during a shutdown**, at weekends and during holidays. However, we know that before long, we are at risk of breakdown, because we haven't carried out essential repairs and maintenance.

One of the reservations I get from my clients when it comes to cutting back on their hours, is that they have too much to do, in too short a timescale and therefore convince themselves that they have to work excessive hours – but all the time. I understand entirely that there are times when it's all hands on deck and that you are required to work longer hours and that's OK – provided it is now and then.

Your Production Plan

If you were a factory manager, you would have a production plan. You would know how much product you could make at any one time, how long the team would have to work to make it and when the shutdowns were going to be for repairs and maintenance. Knowing all of this helps the factory manager identify when he or she can deliver a customer's product.

Imagine, however, if they said yes to all orders without any reference to what was already scheduled to be made. This would mean some delivery deadlines would invariably get missed, the operatives would have to work permanent overtime.

Do you remember me telling you about crying in my PJ's when I first set up my business? I had no production plan. I hadn't worked out what time I needed to effectively run Beee. Now I know that I need half the week client-facing, half the week running the business. I block the time out in my diary and see clients every other day. Several days on the trot training, facilitating or coaching is too tiring. I don't perform at my best. I'm not as sharp as I could be. I don't shine. This also links to the 4-hour rule.

ACTION:

To assist with your production plan:

- What are the main functions of your job? For example, the larger chunks of my role include client meetings or events, product development, finance and marketing.
- If you were to draw a pie chart representing 100% of your working week, how would you ideally divide this time between these main functions?
- Next, review your diary for the last 4 weeks and compare this with your pie chart. What do you need to do differently? For example, if you've spent 3 weeks on the road at sales meetings, what's happening to the other office-based tasks? How could you pace your diary in the future?

Choc-a-Block

I used to wince as I heard myself say, 'Sorry, my diary is choc-a-block.' Conveniently, for this book, the term choc-a-block comes from the nautical world meaning that the tackle blocks are too close together. My diary being choc-a-block is a sign that I have not been spacing appointments out sufficiently enough. This includes both social and work appointments.

How many of us run appointments back to back, including in the evenings and at weekends? If you've got kids, one of the things you can do for them is stop ferrying them around to lots of organised play / hobby / sporting activities. What are we unconsciously teaching young humans about work-life? Not to rest. Not to experience those gaps in time (boredom / relaxation) where we must be resourceful and create our own fun. To be constantly 'on'. To be busy.

We book out every other weekend to ourselves as a family and limit daughter's activities to the week so that we can escape to our boat if we want to. It helps us to rest, stay well, be connected and appreciate our home. It prevents us from being choc-a-block.

I also book out time in my work diary, half the week I am client-facing, the other half of the week I am running my business – this is my admin time...or skiving off to the spa with my friend time.

ACTION:

- What changes would enhance the way you manage your social and work diary?
- What blocks of time would it be useful to carve out in your social and work diary, keeping in mind your earlier Production Plan? Set recurring appointments where possible to save brain calories. Move chunks of time around so that you're not too rigid with folk.

The above habit requires real discipline but is what will keep you running a tight Ship and effectively pacing and managing your production line so that it doesn't break down.

Managing Your Production Line

Being a workaholic experiencing imposter syndrome means that we give ourselves too much to do. That's right, it is our fault. No employer forces us to do anything. We vote with our feet every day by showing up and saying yes through our actions. We:

- **Fail to delegate, negotiate expectations and be realistic** about what we can deliver.
- **Accept the burden of additional work**, because we're good eggs.
- **Do more to feel good about ourselves** and keep the imposter feelings at bay.
- **Feel knowledgeable** when people ask our advice, so willingly give it...and our time.

If we are going to *run a tight ship*, we need to learn to stop putting unnecessary things on the production line in the first place.

When I was employed by the boss from hell, I got myself into a hot stressy mess. Firstly, I felt overwhelmed by the 20 emails containing actions she'd sent whilst I was in bed asleep. Lots of wild ideas she'd identified in the middle of the night – I never knew what to take seriously. I would organise my day by whatever instructions she barked at me over her desk, as opposed to creating a to-do list and negotiating my priorities.

These days I like tasks on my phone. I save brain calories by knowing that my jobs are captured. The minute I remember to do something, I add it to my phone, because I tend to have it with me. Deadlines don't bite me on the bum because I schedule time for project work and have target dates for all my tasks. These pop up on my watch. I also use Alexa to create a shopping list, (she can do task lists too). The family uses it to add items which we are about to run out of. They know if it's not on the list it won't get bought. This shares the burden of having to remember *everything*. Running a tight ship, being organised and having systems prevents firefighting, triggering our stress response and stops us from panicking like Mr Mannering.

ACTION:
- Where, when and with whom do you need to be managing deadline expectations or being more realistic about what you can deliver?
- What are you failing to delegate?
- What gets in the way of you delegating? Often, it's one or a combination of the following:
  - **The need to control**. This is where I see leaders go under. They sink. Their team members' growth

is stunted, and everyone is miserable. Learn to relinquish control.

- **The need to perfect**, because we are the *only* ones that can do that task, correctly, right? Nobody else could possibly learn to do it our way. What is the right way, anyway? Your way? Who says it is right? If the outcome is achieved, does it matter?
- **We don't have time** to show anyone how to do it and say it's easier to do it ourselves. Really? What if nobody showed us when we were starting out?

- How do you know what you have to do each day, week, month, year? How could you capture your to-do's in one spot, which you review regularly?
- How can you get over the above problems? Clue: just do it. Another clue: raise awareness of why you behave the way you do.

An example of a belief which may be an obstacle to your new tight Ship habits would be, 'Everything must be right. I can't afford to get things wrong and if I do, I am a failure.' This belief then leads to perfectionist tendencies and the need to be in control. If you were able to get to the root cause memory which created this belief, you could Haven it away, to help support your behaviour change. Ta daaa!

Saying Yes When You Mean No

To manage our production line, we need to raise our awareness of what we are saying yes to either consciously or unconsciously both at home and at work. Whenever I deliver either assertiveness or time management training, I talk about the importance of being able to say no. Often we don't like to say no because we:

- Don't want to disappoint or let anyone down.
- Like to please and don't want to offend.

- Alternatively, we might tell ourselves 'anything for an easier life' because of a fear of conflict. But is it easier?

Whilst dropping our daughter off at nursery, one of the parents who had a reputation for getting everyone else to look after their kids and not returning the favour, asked me if I would like their elder child to come along to my daughter's fourth birthday party to 'assist'. In the olden days, I would have automatically and unconsciously said yes, to avoid offending. However, (and it has taken a lot of practice), I used my polite and honest policy. I thanked them for their offer and said that I would need to get my head down organising games and food and having an extra child to give jobs to, would give me another job to do. One of the other parents gave me a knowing nod.

My mum uses a brilliant phrase that I say to myself to keep my yeses in check: 'If they're cheeky enough to ask, you're cheeky enough to say no'.

ACTION:
- Reflect on a recent yes that you wanted to say no to.
- What impact did this have on your emotional state – how did you feel about it?
- What effect did it have on your to-do's?
- How much time did it take to do?
- What else could you have done in that time?
- Identify your childhood triggers which cause you to say yes and then Haven them away.
- It can help to have some pre-rehearsed 'no's' at your fingertips. I find the following structure useful:
  - **Be polite: acknowledge their position / thank them for their offer**, e.g. 'Thanks for the offer.'
  - **Be honest: state your position**, e.g. 'To be honest, I'm going to need to get my head down organising the rest of the party and having one extra child to

give jobs to, gives me another job to do.'
- **Zip it. Don't fill the silence.** Smile. Breathe. Allow the conversation to move on. Don't start justifying your position. Stand your ground. Own your spot.

Saying no used to make me feel selfish. In the above example, I didn't feel like a total cow-bag, as their daughter was coming to the party. I was, however, putting our needs first. Hey, I wanted to be able to watch my daughter having fun. To be in what I was in, with her. They're not little forever. Saying yes to the extra child would have meant saying no to the time that I had planned on giving to my daughter and her immediate friends. Plus, I'm not a great multi-tasker.

Once we say yes to a job it's on the production line and has to be managed until it comes off at the other end.

Time Stealers

I can remember a friend saying to me, 'How do you get time to read?' We're back to Parkinson's Law, it's how we choose to spend our time. Do you remember me saying that one of my limiting beliefs about writing this book, was that I didn't think I would have enough time? I had to relook at how I was allocating my time, otherwise, I would have been choc-a-block.

I must admit, I have been sporting the 'dragged through a bush backwards' look and gave up straightening my hair. I have also spent less time chatting at the school gates, but interestingly, I've not had to pull all-nighters or early mornings to get my book written. This is in a year when the business has increased by 15%, I've vlogged most weeks and increased my following by 25%.

We all have the same 24 hours at our disposal. However, sometimes we get dragged into stuff that is just noise, takes us away from Destination Joy and gives us extra things to do. For example, WhatsApp groups. I found myself picking up the phone to see 40 notifications and I'd only been away for a couple of hours. Nonsense stuff about 'how do I deal with a frog in my garden?'. I don't know, let it hop away? I can be an unsociable git, but it was giving me extra tasks to do, so I ejected myself.

ACTION:

Which unnecessary distractions are stealing your time? Here are some examples for consideration:

- **Facebook** or any other social media platform. How much time do you want to spend on social media? Our daughter has a usage time limit on her phone, so that specific apps stop working after 2 hours.
- **Certain people.** When I started work in the legal industry, I discovered that some people use 30 words instead of three. Be like my old boss Bob, he was one of the most efficient fee earners in the business. He also used fewer words. He did strictly 9 – 5 pm and hit all his targets. If you asked for 5 minutes, you got 5 minutes when it suited him and at 4 minutes and 50 seconds, he would start to look at his watch, which was a sign that your time was up and you were about to be dismissed. It was pretty harsh sometimes, and I do think there is a balance, but he was also super-impressive, and people respected his boundaries. You would never give Bob a job that wasn't his.
- **Interruptions from both humans and machine.** Silence your pings and any visual cues. A study identified that it takes us on average, 23 minutes and 15 seconds to get back into our work, once we've been interrupted.[39] Who or what interrupts you? Consider having an interruption slot, so that team members can save up their queries and, in the meantime, they may grow from the experience and discover the solution themselves.

- **Binge-watching TV**. We have Netflix to thank for this. My guilty pleasure – the Real Housewives series. Staying up late steals restorative sleep time, which is one of the most important things for your health, state of mind and performance the next day. More about this in the last chapter.
- **Messages - junk mail, cc-ing to cover a backside, WhatsApp groups.** An oldie but a goodie. I sort my inbox by the sender to spot abusers, do a mass delete and either have a quiet word or unsubscribe. My phone is on silent most of the time and I turn it over so that I can't see the screen. I check in on messages at the start, middle and end of the day. Who are your serial offenders? What could you do differently?
- **Unfocused, un-purposeful, actionless meetings.** Enough said. Cancel it. Chair it (to take charge of it, but otherwise don't add another unnecessary job) or send apologies.

Ask yourself these test questions before you get rid of any to-dos:

- Does this activity take me closer to Destination Joy?
- If not, does the task itself simply bring me joy or relaxation and is not going to drastically jeopardise me reaching my vision? If so, keep it!
- What are your time stealing activities? What could you ditch or cut back on?

People Boundaries

So, we've looked at time boundaries, we also need to consider our people boundaries too. A boundary is an imaginary line that we set for ourselves in terms of how we allow people to treat us and often there can be connections to our values and beliefs.

I used to be a complete doormat. It was fine for people to walk all over me; I would dust myself off and continue to be loyal. I would allow others to be disrespectful and unkind and would simply retreat away from the 'bad' behaviour. I would stay quiet and stay hurt.

One of the things I hear myself saying to my clients when they tell me about how someone has treated them is, 'That's not OK is it?' They often look at me like I've slapped them with a wet fish. They have been so used to unconsciously accepting the 'bad' behaviour from others that it doesn't seem to register on their radar.

So, what do I mean by 'bad' behaviour? There are certain behaviours which put me on alert to manage my boundaries, for example, when someone is:

- **Over-controlling**. A previous boss used to ask what I had been doing in the toilet, (catching 5 minutes with my best mate if the truth be told). She would also try to get me to change my notes from disciplinary hearings and would say things like, 'Are you sure the line manager said that?' Her behaviour would trigger me to doubt myself.

- **Manipulative**. They sew the seed of something which they think needs to be done and know that because you are the responsible type, you will pick up the gauntlet and run with it. They drop hints, play the victim and give reasons as to why they cannot deal with the matter themselves. Before you know it, you've added another job to your production line and often, it's a crappy one.

- **Aggressive or rude**. I used to be scared of anyone who showed me aggression and would freeze, let alone be able to stand my ground and open my mouth. Whilst on a trip up north I bumped into an old work colleague that I had helped through a difficult time. They'd been having mental health issues. My guard was down and with hindsight, she was doing the whole smiling assassin thing. I didn't detect what was about to come – a public dressing down. I naively thought she wanted me to help her again.

She told me she was annoyed with me and that I had not provided her with enough support. You could argue she was using her honesty policy, but she wasn't being polite. She was distorting the facts.

I had spent hours listening and coaching her through her problems (for free), signposted her to various resources. Nobody else in her support network had done this. She was being unfair, so I calmly reminded her of the facts. I was very honest and polite. She crossed the line. She lost my loyalty. I know I'd been generous with my time and had given enough of myself. Enough was enough.

- **Selfish, one-way street, takers**. You know the sort. They fail to pay up when the bill is presented. They don't return dinner invitations. They disappear when it is time to clear the dishes. They 'forget' to bring their gift. They expect you to do all the running and then moan because they don't see enough of you. They look after number one. They are interested in what they can get from a person or establishment. The relationship is one-way. It is such a shame as they are missing out on the real pleasure of balanced giving to others.

Boundary Management Solutions:
- Call out the behaviour. Use tangible, specific examples of what you have seen and heard, (with your own eyes and ears, not hearsay – the facts) and explain how it makes you feel. Then agree how you'd like things to be instead.
- Use the polite and honest policy.
- If the relationship is unbalanced, take corrective action.

Ask for what you need and if they are not forthcoming, withdraw whatever it was that you were giving and move on!

- Step away from the relationship if needs be or reduce your exposure. Life is short my friend. Spend your time wisely and where possible on the things that bring you joy.

ACTION:

- What behaviours directed towards you have not been OK? Who crosses the line?
- What boundaries are being breached?
- What people boundaries do you need to set and with whom?
- Which of the above boundary management solutions could you use?

Owning Your Space

To support our boundaries, it's important to give off an alternative vibe, so that people know you mean business. We need to own our space.

One of the things I notice with this client group is that they minimise themselves physically by making their bodies smaller, by contracting themselves and closing their body language. They minimise themselves mentally by adopting imposter syndrome thoughts and not believing they are good enough. They also minimise themselves linguistically in the way they interact with others, but worst of all, they allow others to minimise them.

Have you ever experienced a situation when someone enters yours 'space' and you feel knocked out of the way, even though they haven't physically touched you? I can remember being on holiday in Halkidiki. I'd finished walking on the beach barefoot and was washing the sand off my feet. A fellow holidaymaker barged metaphorically into my space as opposed to waiting in the queue, (I know I'm so British).

Her action made me feel hurried and as though I needed to move out of the way, as her needs were more pressing. I turned to see what the emergency was; there wasn't one. The old me would have scarpered out of the way so that she could occupy the space in which I was standing. Instead, I acknowledged her, held her gaze and carried on. My husband would have taken extra time, intricately washing his feet – he's great at owning his space.

I get regular requests from HR Directors to help a member of staff to be more confident. Take Harry, a lawyer who'd been sent for coaching because he was giving the wrong impression to his clients. Technically he was very able, but he was giving off the wrong vibes, which undermined the impression he gave to clients. His lack of confidence made his clients lack confidence in the advice he was giving.

Linguistically he would undermine and minimise himself by over-apologising, using 'just', 'kind of' and 'do you know what I mean?' He would obsessively touch his cuff links and face. These are known as reassurance gestures. Prince Charles taps his handkerchief pocket and cuff links before entering a public arena.

He had no armpit space as I like to call it. His arms were packed tightly against his body. His knees, shins and feet were also clenched together. His chin was dipped so that his eye contact looked submissive. He wasn't owning his space. This guy wanted to be a partner one day but was damaging his credibility as perceived by others. His potential wasn't shining through.

ACTION:

- How do you minimise yourself linguistically? What verbal junk could you get rid of?
- When, where and with whom do you physically move

out of the way for others?

- What causes you to do this? What are your underlying beliefs?
- Are there any connected events from your childhood which need Havening?
- If you were to physically own your space, what would you be doing differently?

Can you remember Mark from Chapter 1 – the exec who wanted more presence in the boardroom? He stopped undermining himself linguistically by deleting the word 'sorry' from his vocabulary – unless of course he genuinely needed to apologise. We got rid of the limiting beliefs from his childhood which made him 'invisible'.

He took positive steps to begin owning his space. He prepared himself for meetings, by arriving early and sitting in a position where he could get the CEO's attention, as opposed to sitting back away from the rest of the group. He broadened out his physiology and his personal possessions (notebook, papers etc), giving the impression of confidence, whilst also making himself feel better.

Gone was the small scrunched up hedgehog-like physiology, which made it easier for him to be ignored. He stopped being the chief note-taker, which meant he got a more realistic proportion of the actions. He stopped being the good egg who ensured everyone had their cup of tea. He brought his giving and receiving back into balance. He let others take a turn. He was able to raise the important matters that he previously couldn't find his voice for. He physically and mentally claimed his space at the table.

Be Mindful of the Gap

Mark was a firstborn and had got into the habit of feeling obliged to fill the gaps, through the unconscious messages he was given as a child by his parents. I coach a high proportion of firstborns. When you look at the firstborn theory, they are used to being responsible because of being left to their own devices. They learn how to take care of themselves and their younger siblings. This level of responsibility taking stays with the adult. Any theory is a generalisation and I appreciate that not all families fit within this dynamic. I have coached many responsible middle, last and only borns too.

Because we continue to fill the gaps, people continue to let us! For example, there were folk in my life that I would routinely call and maintain contact with. They didn't call me, because, at an unconscious level, they knew that before long I would pick up the phone, facetime or make arrangements to see them. I changed this policy a few years ago, and do you know what, some of those relationships have gone by the wayside. This hurt at first, but it taught me that there has to be give and take, not take, take, take. Otherwise, we're giving ourselves more things to do!

We get a reputation for being responsible, people know unconsciously through our past patterns of behaviour that we're great at getting a job done, (and for being busy and stressed). When I facilitate team sessions, there are always certain characters that can be relied upon when we get to the action planning phase; they are the first to nominate themselves for the tasks. Whereas others will happily sit back, not take any actions themselves and then designate other people that aren't in the room! And that's because they know they won't kick up a fuss when they find out. Unconsciously the good eggs have been picking up the tab for other people's work when others are not forthcoming.

Take Nigel for example, who'd been unconsciously saying yes to his team for years. He was a highly capable executive running a business employing over 250 people. He wouldn't think anything of clearing cups and equipment after a meeting, whilst the rest of the team scarpered and left him to it.

Now, I'm all for leaders, leading by example. However, I'm not for people being taken advantage of. Equally, I am not suggesting that you become a lazy leader either. However, if we focus on doing the right things – the important results or outputs we are employed to deliver in a role – the things that make us a 'success'; we shine more.

Sometimes we need to re-brand ourselves through our actions, so that we get known for being something different, preventing people from unconsciously taking advantage of us. Be more like Bob.

ACTION:
- When do you fill the responsibility gaps?
- What messages does your behaviour communicate about your personal brand? What are you known for?
- What are you going to do differently? Go on, I dare you to be a little less responsible for other people's crap!

When I challenged Nigel, he said, 'Well, it only took me 10 minutes.' However, those were 10 minutes which could have been shared by the rest of the team and took him away from managing his business; it also re-enforced his 'you can take advantage of me' brand. Ten minutes here and there soon add up over the days, weeks and years. When coachees protest, I ask them to work out their hourly rate and establish how much it costs their business. We then work out how else that time could be used.

Recognise When You've Used Up Your Help Quotient

I could be a full-time professional coffee drinker and free coaching business mentor. I wouldn't make any money out of it... I used to be the one out of pocket because I didn't like to be stingy and found it hard to let others pay.

I recently got a request for coffee via LinkedIn from a Life Coach. She said looking at my profile, she thought there was 'a lot of synergy'. I didn't think so when I reviewed her profile and listened to her long pushy voice message. She was working in a very different market and selling services that were unrelated to mine. I used my honest and polite policy and tried to help by suggesting she contact someone in my network, whom I thought she would have this magical 'synergy' with.

She persisted. Three long meandering and slightly sarcastic messages later, (did she really think we were going to meet up after that?!), it called for my really honest and polite policy.

Last year I realised I'd used up my help quotient and chose to use my time differently to write this book. For almost 8 years I volunteered for my local CIPD (Chartered Institute of Personnel and Development) and trained and mentored the branch members to be coaches for free.

I did it because I love the industry and when I was developing as an HR professional, I paid to be mentored through my exams, so would have loved the free service which we were providing. Additionally, it floated my professional boat. I love seeing people grow and develop, it makes my hairs stand on end and sometimes moves me to tears. After agonising for months over the decision, I gave this role up.

ACTION:
- Where are you exceeding your help quotient?
- What are you going to do about it?

Now, do I ever go out for coffee? I sure do. I have a lovely network of clients and associates that I go and chew the cud with BUT there is a fair exchange of information and business! You know, balanced giving and taking. If you're in any doubt as to whether you're benefiting from a meeting or how you are allocating your time, ask yourself:

- What's the purpose?
- What's in it for them?
- What's in it for me?
- What will be the positive and negative consequence of me giving this time away?
- Will this use of time bring me joy, (this is your get-out clause if you really can't justify spending the time)?

The LinkedIn Life Coach eventually got the message. I said that I didn't think there was any synergy, which was why I recommended she contact someone else. I don't like having to be really honest and polite, however, some people have the skin of a rhinoceros. They are unable to pick up on the subtle cues which are being communicated and carry on badgering you regardless. If I'd met up with her so that I didn't offend, I would have resented it. That resentment would have caused tension in my body and I would have lost valuable time.

Dealing with the Life Coach required me to manage both my time and people boundaries. Practising both these disciplines means you'll *run a tight ship*. It will give you more time to do the important things, less stress because you won't have unnecessary to-dos and you'll be able to focus on delivering the things that make you shine.

Summary of Key Points:
- Work fills the time we give it. We all have the same 24 hours a day. Create work time boundaries.
- If we are to optimise our performance and enhance our shine, we need to restrict our thinking time to 4 hours.
- Manage your production line by restricting what goes on it in the first place by saying no, delegating and not taking responsibility for tasks that aren't yours. Stop filling the gaps.
- Understand your production plan. What can you

realistically produce in the time you have? How much time do you need to do all the elements of your job?

- Schedule recurring blocks of time to help slow your production line down. Don't be choc-a-block with appointments running back to back. Apply the same rules to your personal diary too. Even the most extraverted need downtime. If you're tired, your shine is dulled, and you won't perform at your best.

- Be like Bob. Manage your people boundaries. This will help to re-brand how you are perceived and what people can and cannot get away with. Use the honest and polite policy.

- Recognise when you've used up your help quotient. Ask yourself what you stand to gain and lose and analyse whether it's worth it.

Chapter 8

Antidote #8: Develop Your Inner Captain

If you have good thoughts they will shine out your face like sunbeams and you will always look lovely.
Roald Dahl

One of the things I have noticed about the clients that don't fully transform themselves is that they fail to get to grips with their inner critic and thinking. It's our inner critic that makes us feel like an imposter, which can then cause us to over-work and get stressed. They also continue to fall foul of the thinking traps which keep them stuck, such as feeling like a victim, turning persecutor or worrying; not recognising that they are the Captain of their thoughts and the custodian of their belief system. They continue to succumb to 'I've got to work hard all the time' or 'I'm not good enough' deliberations.

In this chapter, I'm going to provide you with strategies that will shrink imposter thoughts and help you to develop a more positive and flexible mindset. You'll also be able to deal with the curveballs of work-life. However, probably what's most important is that you use these strategies as part of your 'maintenance' going forward, as they will enhance your joy and deter the doldrums.

You are going to learn how to become your own cheerleader as opposed to being 'Debbie Downer', (a Saturday Night Live character who frequently adds bad news and negative feelings). You'll learn how to direct an alternative script in your head, using your Inner Captain and their various supporting characters. You'll also discover some antidotes to the doldrums, which will help add more joy to your work-life.

So, to recap your unconscious mind acts as your Autopilot.

Your Autopilot received most of its programming between the ages of 0-7. These programmes enable you to act without conscious thought. This is why we target Havening in these early years – to change the automatic programmes that are hindering us.

Each programme has its own associated language pattern. When I work with my clients I intensively listen to their words so that I can get to the root cause in their childhood. You can make significant and magical shifts with Havening. However, some things are that unconscious that it can be difficult to find the root cause. This is where the thinking strategies that follow can help.

Your unconscious mind is processing everything you are not consciously aware of right now. What's interesting is that your unconscious mind is always listening. It's processing the words you use both in your head and with other people – not to mention the words you write, read and hear – hence why you can feel drained having spent time with someone negative.

We can at least take charge of our thoughts by embracing our Inner Captain and ensuring that the messages and direction given by our Captain, positively programme our Ship towards our desired destination. To a certain degree, you can also control what you see and hear too. Remember the production line in Chapter 7? Well, I also like to think of our mind as a factory. We have:

- Inputs at one end (raw materials) – our thoughts and language
- Process in the middle (machinery) – our unconscious mind
- Output at the other end (product) – our state, which triggers our behaviour, actions and ultimately the results we are getting

ACTION:

Let's try some language processing experiments:

- Read out the following statements slowly:
  - 'I'm *not* going to eat that delicious, sticky toffee pudding and vanilla custard, which is sat there on the counter steaming away, begging to be devoured.'
    - What did you start thinking about? Did you get a picture, sound, feeling, smell or taste? (If you hate sticky toffee pudding, try swapping it with a naughty treat that you love).
  - 'I'm going to prepare some healthy vegetable snacks I can grab from the fridge when I get hungry at 3.30 pm.'
    - What did you start thinking about?
    - This statement is written to leverage success. It is the small step moving towards the destination of e.g. eating more healthily, as opposed to visualising yourself being slimmer, which would be the final outcome. This reinforces what I was saying in Chapter 5 about visualising.
- Next, write down your definition of happiness ensuring everything is *stated positively* and is not a list of things you don't want.
  - Read it out aloud slowly. How did it make you feel? What pictures, sounds, feelings, smell or tastes did it generate?

Most of our processing is below conscious awareness, but hopefully, you are beginning to tune into that processing having completed the above exercises. So, what happens when we focus on negative words and thoughts?

The Impact of Negative Thoughts and Language

In a series of studies highlighted in a Psychology Today

article[40] using negative language can have negative biological consequences for us, which can ultimately result in a shorter, less successful and joy-filled life. In one study seeing a list of negative words for a few seconds will make an anxious and depressed person feel worse. If they continue to ruminate, they begin to damage the structures that regulate memory, feelings and emotions.[41]

In another study, our brain responds to fearful thoughts, for example about death, even when they're not real, as though they are occurring in the outside world. This triggers a response from our thalamus and amygdala.[42]

Now, here's the kicker when it comes to reframing our thinking and using more positive language; we have a neural bias for negativity. This is a survival mechanism and harks back to the days when there were countless threats to our existence. To overcome this neural bias, Fredrickson and Losada recommend that we express five positive thoughts for each expression of negativity.[43] The great news is that positive words and thoughts drive the motivational centres of the brain into action and help us to be more resilient when faced with problems in work-life.[44]

ACTION:

- Identify a topic that you typically moan about. It could be a person, place, policy, company – there are no rules, other than it must hack you off a little.
- Next, write down in one sentence why it gets your goat. Notice how this makes you feel.
- Now write down 5 positive thoughts to counter the negative sentence. Tune into how this makes you feel.
- What are you going to do differently?

Your Inner Captain

The role of your Inner Captain is to keep your thoughts in check; to re-frame negativity; to be objective and practical; to support you positively and compassionately, but also be firm sometimes.

Probably one of the most challenging times of my life was being diagnosed with cancer; initially, my Inner Captain went AWOL for a few days. I had to roll out all my tools to get myself back on track.

I'd feared cancer since I was a little girl and was haunted by memories of a little boy called Ben who got leukaemia. We watched his suffering on the news for months. Then the poor little thing died. It was heartbreaking to watch and taught me that cancer meant death and suffering. When I realised this, guess what I did? I Havened away the memories. They were unhelpful in this context.

I went to get my moles checked out. The GP I saw can either be extremely helpful and knowledgeable or brusque and demeaning. It's potluck. I only ever go to this person if I am desperate and there are no other doctors available.

I self-consciously disrobe and show them the offending moles. They laughed in a superior, all-knowing, you're wasting my time way and told me I was simply getting old. They were 'just age spots'. I tried to forget the experience, but then several months later, whilst I was running a course, I couldn't stop scratching my back. I asked my husband to look; he said he couldn't see anything, but I did have a funny-looking mole.

I didn't want to risk the humiliation a second time, so did what GP's have told me they hate us doing when I've trained them; I Googled it. I self-diagnosed. I downloaded a mole checking app called 'Skin Vision'. You take a picture of your mole and the algorithm tells you whether it is 'high risk' or not. It said that 'there is some similarity between your photo and the skin cancer images on our database'.

I dashed off to our 'gym' in our garage. I didn't want my daughter to get wind of what was going on and needed a good cry. Immediately my mind went to the worst-case scenario – to everything I'd scared myself with on the internet. I'd filled my head with horror stories, such as if it was melanoma, the nasty kind, it could spread to other areas of the body and you could die from it. All I could think about was not being able to be there for my girl growing up and leaving the love of my life to cope with it all. I'd not even been formally diagnosed yet.

I stump up the courage to go back to the doctors and I'm referred immediately to see an amazing consultant. He manages my expectations by saying, '9/10 moles are not cancerous.' This was one of the things I kept repeating to myself. It grounded me. It reminded me of the facts. By this time my 'Inner Captain' had kicked in and I was being more disciplined with myself as to where I was allowing my thoughts to wander.

ACTION:

- If something is currently playing on your mind, (please avoid creating worrying thoughts, if you're not worried about something, skip this step), what are the facts in this scenario?
- What could you repeatedly say to yourself that would help you to feel more grounded about this situation?

Because we can control some thoughts, can't we? For example, every time you meet someone, do you think about them carrying out their ablutions? Nope! How about the moment you were conceived? Urrgh! Sorry about that. You might now be considering those points having read them. This is how we programme our minds, but more on that later. Go on, distract yourself from these thoughts. I'll explain how, next.

Blackpool Illuminations

Going to Blackpool Illuminations was one of the highlights of our year. We'd go on a double-decker bus, buy glowsticks, eat fish and chips, wear 'Kiss Me Quick' hats and wait in anticipation for the first bulb to be switched on. Then before we knew it, the whole promenade was lit up. I think of negative thoughts in a similar way.

One thought leads to one light going off in your head. Then before you know it, you're lost in a chain of negativity and you have a whole string of lights lit up in your head! This then results in a body and mind full of negative chemicals brewing inside, which can last for ages. The trick is being able to spot when the first lightbulb goes on and then, interrupting the pattern of thought so that you're not faced with Blackpool Illuminations! There are various things you can do:

- **Become a master of distraction**, as referred to in previous chapters. Use this technique for low grade, insignificant but irritating thoughts. Examples of distraction could include, watching a comedy, going for a mindful walk, (where you use your senses), reading something positive or enthralling.
- **Tell the thought to stop,** again, providing it is low-grade stuff. I use my Mrs Whiplash voice (more about her later) and simply say 'Stop' to the thought. I have also been known to sing, the chorus from Disney's Frozen 'Let It Go' sequence performed by Idina Menzel.
- **Don't use distraction or suppress thoughts**, if a thought needs to be processed, use *The Inner Brilliance, Outer Shine Journal* (more on this later) and work it out in your journal.
- **Use EFT** (Emotional Freedom Technique). If I've had a crappy day and really can't seem to shift my thinking, I tap it out whilst walking my dogs around the deserted fields where we live. I cover this in the next chapter.
- If it's a recurring, persistent thought, chances are it's an old thought, i.e. something from your childhood. **Go**

and find the source and Haven it away. I can always tell when a client issue has been dealt with – their language changes. The issue is no longer present in the words they use.

What If-ing and Plan B

Even though the consultant had reassured me, I still had 'What if?' questions. What if questions can send us into a blind panic. They can make us catastrophise. They trigger our stress response. Whenever I find myself what if-ing, I get real. I get practical. I work out how I would cope in the event of the worst-case scenario happening. What would my 'Plan B' be? Somehow this frees me from worry because I work out how I could handle a problem. Your calm Inner Captain takes charge.

ACTION:

- You know that worry from earlier if you are what if-ing, what could your Plan B be?
- What are the practical steps you could take to cope with this situation?

Continuing the theme of being practical, I wanted to know what would happen next if the mole was cancerous. The consultant looked at me with trepidation and then slight annoyance that his 9/10 speech hadn't pacified me. I reassured him that knowing more helped me to be level-headed and prepare myself mentally. He explained that the next step would be to have a minor operation to have it removed so that they could check to see what type of cancer it was. I was so relieved. I thought *I can handle that*.

I didn't want to know anything else at that stage. I stopped googling. My next reassuring Inner Captain phrase which kept me sane was, *I'll cross that bridge when I get to it*.

ACTION:

- Concerning your earlier worry, identify what reassuring Inner Captain phrases you could use.

- If you don't have a worry, what negative or critical things do you say to yourself? How do your imposter syndrome thoughts work? What do you say to yourself which causes you to overwork?

- What compassionate, reassuring, pragmatic things could you say to yourself instead? I find it helps to prepare ahead of time, stock phrases you can roll out when you need them. One of my other examples is, *What is said is said. What is done is done.* I use this statement if I ever catch myself re-winding the tape of a conversation.

- The tone of voice you use with yourself is also important here. If you were to use a critical, hurried, impatient, angry or worried tone with your statement, it won't have a positive effect, but more about this later on when we look at the different characters you can employ.

A letter arrived from the hospital and it was time to cross that bridge! I'd been told I would get a letter discharging me if things were OK. I'd been invited in for another appointment; not good news then. My Inner Captain went AWOL again for half an hour. I went into a blind panic thinking worst-case scenario again. I rang my husband and then my mum and cried lots. It's good to release emotions, but more about that in the next chapter.

Then the Captain kicked in again and I realised I needed to take charge of the situation. I didn't have all the facts. I was making assumptions. I rang the hospital. I will always be grateful to the kind receptionist who uttered these words to me, 'Sorry love. If you've been called back in, it means the mole is dodgy.' She probably shouldn't have told me that, but I appreciated it so much. I had more facts. I could prepare myself mentally for my appointment.

Fear of the unknown can be scary. When we are fearful, we can end up making all sorts of horror movies in our mind. Playing out a script that hasn't even happened yet.

Useful or Use-less Thoughts?

How often do we consider whether our thoughts are useful or useless? One of my first gifts from my husband when we started dating, was a book about worry. I was in shock! His nickname for me was, 'My little worrit'. Was I really that bad?

Then he wafted, *Feel The Fear And Do It Anyway: How to Turn Your Fear and Indecision into Confidence and Action* by Susan Jeffers[45] under my nose – another hint. I read it and said, 'Am I really that negative?' He looked at me anxiously having been asked one of those questions that could end in trouble either way. He swallowed hard and said 'Erm...yes sometimes.' Well, that was a revelation. Sat here chuckling.

I had no Bridge; I wasn't particularly self-aware back then. I learnt to feel the fear and do it anyway. It revolutionised my life. I started to believe that anything was possible. So much so, that I thought everyone else should read the book. I bought and distributed copies to my family and friends. Not everyone wanted to be helped. I had to learn to keep my newfound positivity to myself...or at least be less 'Rod, Jane and Freddie' about it.

ACTION:

- What are you afraid of doing that you haven't dared to do yet and is this part of your Vision?
- How would you feel if you got to the end of your life, having not done the thing you are currently afraid of doing?
- What are you going to do about it? (Be the Brave Captain).
- What use-less thoughts do you have about this?
- What thoughts would be more useful?

- What would be the very first step that you could take within the next 24 hours? Remember the swimming pool analogy in Chapter 5? Take it bit by bit. Micro step, by micro-step.

I once went on a 'Positive Thinking' course with a colleague from work. We were used to grunting our good mornings in the kitchen whilst we made our first coffee of the day. However, after that training we would say in jest, 'How are you today?', the response was always something over the top and cheesy like, 'I'm positively marvellous!' We laughed about it, because we were very sceptical and thought it couldn't possibly make us feel better, but do you know what, it did!

Usually, when I got home and my husband asked me how my day was, I would take a deep intake of breath and then launch into telling him everything that was wrong with it. He would start to glaze over within about 30 seconds. He knew that I was going to moan about the same old things. Groundhog day! But following this course and another great book *How to be Brilliant. Change Your Ways in 90 Days!* by Michael Heppell[46], I trained myself to focus on what had gone well and to talk about that instead. It wasn't that I didn't mention the crappy stuff but what changed is that I slowly developed my Inner Captain and used the resources that follow, which meant that the negative things were less prominent – because I took charge. I no longer had to burden him with every single worried thought that entered my head.

Down in the Doldrums

Being in the doldrums came to refer specifically to sailing ships that were stuck and unable to progress. Today it has come to mean in a state of stagnation, lacking activity, feeling blue or depressed.

I can honestly say that I have only ever felt depressed (as a fully-fledged adult having learnt these techniques), once. It was following our last attempt at IVF. We'd agreed that if it failed a third time having used up all our embryos that we would stop. During our last attempt, I got the dreaded call. The embryo had died. For 6 weeks I mourned the loss of the children we could have had.

Then one day, I woke up and realised that this was the best thing for us. It's amazing what work your unconscious mind can do, whilst you are off-line. I'd been positively processing these feelings. Twisting the scenario this way and that. We were happy as we were. I'd got stuck on a mindless thought train of, *the next thing people do is have baby number two and everybody has two kids in our family.* Not whether this was actually the right thing for us.

We have the most beautiful soul between us and I feel proud of her every day. We were made to be a three. She is absolutely enough for us. We are very lucky to have her – our miracle child. My everything.

Depression does serve a purpose, particularly when we are grieving or have suffered a loss. It's like an enforced shutdown and I think it has a place.

Equally, we can create our own depression by repeatedly re-accessing crappy memories and letting our negative inner critique take hold. If the memories are persistent and you can't shake them off, go and Haven them. Alternatively, find a Havening Practitioner that can help.

I have heard people say that because they are having an off day, they declare it as the start of depression. Once we label ourselves depressed, we own that badge. We lookout for the signs and evidence of depression. We negatively prime our brains to look out for the thing we don't want, because we get more of whatever we focus on. I call this Yellow Car Syndrome. I once had a yellow car. I thought it was unique. Turns out it's not. As I drove it home from the garage, guess what else I noticed? All the other yellow cars on the road. Prime yourself to notice the happy moments instead, even if it is seconds, to begin with.

Negative states of mind are like a bad smell. They come and go. We can hold the duvet tight around us and continue to bask in the rotten ambience or we can loosen our grip and wait for the negative state to dissipate, (or cheat and use EFT in the next chapter).

We have to learn to relax and be easy with ourselves. So, what if you're having an off day. You're entitled. You're human.

ACTION:

- If a bad mood starts to linger, what are you going to do about it?
- What could you do to lift your mood? (You'll get more tools in the next chapter too).

In Johann Harri's's book *Lost Connections: Uncovering the Real Causes of Depression – and the Unexpected Solutions*[47], he talks about the Hamilton Scale which is used for measuring depression. 0 = you are skipping along merrily, through to 51 = you are considering crashing your vehicle into a tree. Johann, a Journalist, New York Times Best Selling Author and TED Talker, had been severely depressed and had taken anti-depressants since he was a teenager, having to continually change his medication and ramp up the dosage.

He was told his brain was imbalanced and set out to prove otherwise in his book. He discovered through research that 'Depression and anxiety are not caused by a chemical imbalance in our brains. In fact, they are largely caused by key problems with the way we live today'.

In his book, he talks about anti-depressants giving a 1.8 point positive shift in the Hamilton Scale. If someone is suicidal, this is where 1.8 points away from committing the act could save someone's life. However, improving your sleeping patterns can give you a 6 point leap! More about sleep in Chapter 10.

Your Inner Captain's Voice

Before I begin, please don't confuse what I am about to say with psychotic disorders such as schizophrenia, where the patient hears vocal hallucinations. I am referring to the mental conversations – the inner dialogue we have with ourselves.

For example, have you ever read an email or a message in a grumpy, huffy voice tone and then misinterpreted what was said? You know, those messages from certain people. The messages you dread. The communications that you convince yourself will be negative. Reading the words in your grumpy voice and then chuntering about it in your head, will only intensify any negative feelings. We're also at risk of distorting the meaning of the communication; like when your partner buys you flowers and you assume they've done something wrong.

Then we share our misery with other people and complain about what has been sent to us. As proof, we read it out to them, but this time, using our best reading voice. Damn and blast, it changes the meaning! The other person looks at us like, 'What are you talking about?'; you swiftly put your phone back in your pocket.

Years ago, when I first started Beee, I used to do phobia cures. I can remember resolving a spider phobia by pretending that the tarantula had a voice, which sounded like Minnie Mouse. You know, high pitched and non-threatening. Changing the tone of your voice changes the meaning.

Think about it for a minute. How did you know you were in trouble growing up? I know my mum used to use a certain tone and somehow extended the length of my name, 'Estelllllllle'. The same applies to the voice in our head. Our Inner Captain's voice.

There are several character voices I use in my head and they all serve a purpose:

- **Mrs Whiplash is my no-nonsense character**. Her voice tone is firm. I use her when I'm being victim-like. She will say, *Get on with it! Enough. Stop Moaning.* My inner whinging time tends to be first thing in the morning when I'm cleaning my teeth. I sometimes slip into giving myself a negative pep talk. So helpful – not! Knowing when your inner moaning time is, generates more information for your Bridge, which your Captain can take advantage of.
- **Mrs Cheerleader**. Her voice tone is positive and compassionate. For example, before I deliver a presentation I am less familiar with, she'll say things like, *Come on; you can do it. You are well-rehearsed. You are good at what you do. You've got this.*
- **Then there's Yoda**, the way he speaks makes me laugh because my husband does a mean Yoda impression. My inner Yoda helps me to see the funny side of work-life; to make light of my mistakes and foibles. Now, this is OK, because I have good self-esteem (now) and embrace my Treasure Trove, which enables me to feel secure enough to take the mickey out of myself. He sounds like, *Letting go of this thought now am I.*[48]

Those characters work for me. You need to get your own set of characters. When I've run this exercise with groups of people they have come up with all sorts of examples including Rocky, Peter Kaye, Margaret Thatcher, and Beyonce. Sometimes it's a teacher or relative who inspired and believed in them growing up. Now, the rule is that you must have at least one compassionate character in your armoury because inner dialogue tends to be very critical, hence the term 'Inner Critic'.

ACTION:

- What type of inner characters do you need?
- Who could represent each of your characters?
- What useful things could they say?

Learn to Take the P Bob

I can be self-deprecating at times. I share with you what's in my head so that you realise that you are normal. We are all fallible and quirky. We all have thoughts about ourselves. The small print is that I can only do this now because I like myself. I appreciate the Miss Stiff Knickers within. I fit somewhere, along with all the other stiff wearing knickers and pants brigade. I think it's hilarious that I am a biff. I don't have a cool bone in my body, but that's OK because it is who I am. I accept myself.

In my experience, the more we try to cover up who we really are, the more transparent we become. People see through our mask. We've only got one body and mind, why not embrace it? Embrace the lumps, the bumps, the imperfections, the intellectual weaknesses. So flipping what! Other people can think what they like, it's what you think about yourself that matters. If you skimped on Chapter 4, which was about embracing your gifts, talents, achievements and getting comfortable with your weakness, go back. Do that work – it's worth it. You're worth it. Blimey, my business is called Beee because I believe in people absolutely beeeing themselves.

ACTION:

- When, where and with whom do you wear a mask / are you not yourself?
- Which part of yourself have you not accepted and embraced yet?
- What's funny about who you are?
- When, where and with whom is it safe to begin showing the lighter side of you?

Reverse Gratitude

One of the things I've noticed with human beings (particularly us Brits), is that we can engage in reverse gratitude, i.e. peering over the fence at the Jones' lawn to check out how green it is and making ourselves miserable in the process. Social media makes this even easier.

Take for example, on a trip to Galicia, Spain to attend my sister's wedding I found myself blown away by the beauty of the area she was living in. I would describe it as a Spanish Cornwall, with a hint of the Lake District. These are two of my favourite places in the UK. Throw into the mix, the fact that my sister has so quickly integrated into such a welcoming community and is renovating a beautiful house, which is surrounded by eucalyptus trees and rolling hills. It's like a piece of heaven.

On the day before the wedding when I arrive at my sister's house, it was buzzing with her friends from all over the world; they were mucking in to prepare the house and banquet. Quiches were being prepared and they realised they needed eggs. At home I would pop 4 minutes down the road in my car to M & S. Galician life is so different. When you want eggs you get them from your neighbours.

My sister puts my niece on her shoulders, the dog is in tow too, happily wandering down a tree-clad traffic-free road. It takes us a good 45 minutes to make the short trip down the lane because the old mammas in their blue checked pinafores come out of their houses to kiss, chat and hug; they do it in an unhurried way and as though they have all the time in the world.

When we get back, another neighbour has been around to deliver a huge basket of homegrown vegetables. Are you jealous yet? It was like the 'Good Life'.

Jealousy isn't a frequent emotion I experience, I think it is because there is nothing that floats my boat more, than seeing people happy and doing well for themselves – it makes me happy too. Also, I believe that if you want something badly enough, you can go and make it happen.

I am by no means perfect. I did do a property search the next day and I overheard my mum saying, 'Estelle and I are looking at property here.' He heee. I got carried away in a fantasy for a few days.

Re-Dipping

I came away from Spain with my body and mind filled with love. Do you know what I mean by that? How does it work for you? For me, it's almost a suspension of judgement, ego and an unconditional positive regard for human beings. I have my rose-tinted glasses on. Everything and everyone is amazing and lovely, as though there are halos and sunshine everywhere.

We have a saying in our family, which is, 'Oo I'm going to live off that memory for days.' My sister's wedding weekend was one of those memories. I've been re-dipping into it all week. Have you ever noticed that we do the reverse of that too? We re-dip into memories that make us feel like crap. We re-play horror movies or worst still, we direct and construct horror movies about events that haven't even occurred yet.

ACTION:

- Which are the recurring horror movies that you torment yourself with? If there is a memory whether real, imagined or is something you dream about, this is an opportunity for Havening. Go on, go and Haven it now!
- Secondly, which are the amazing memories that you need to dust off and re-live? Go get yourself a waft of them. You want to re-dip those. Even better, go and reminisce with the person you shared it with. By accessing positive memories, we fill our bodies up with good chemicals. When we do the opposite, we get the opposite.

Gratitude & Mindfully Seeing

There is plenty in social media about the benefits of gratitude and sometimes an almost passive-aggressive push and guilt trip if you're not grateful for your lot. However, studies show that it does you good. Emmons and McCullough from the Department of Psychology, University of California, found that those that counted their blessings as opposed to their burdens evidenced higher well-being.[49] When I returned from our weekend away in Spain, I was absolutely shattered. Classic introvert: I can only do so much socialising. Towards the end of the weekend, my sister caught me hiding in her cosy kitchen, by the log burner with a cup of tea, sat in my Nana's old chair.

On my first day back at work, the weather in the UK was appalling; cold, dull and wet. We'd transitioned into autumn, way too quickly. It was such a contrast to the glorious sunshine we'd experienced a few days ago on the promenade, overlooking the twinkling turquoise sea with its bobbing fishing boats. I was tired, it was miserable, I was feeling blue because I was missing my sister and I was supposed to be writing this book. As I've been writing, I've learnt that whatever I'm feeling comes out in my fingertips and is translated into words on a page.

I needed another break! I gave myself the day off. I spent the day doing some of the things I love about my life. I'd got a new car and still couldn't drive it properly. I'd spent the previous week kangarooing through the village or screeching out of junctions like I was in a Dukes of Hazard car chase. I'd had to steer clear of the 'dynamic' knob, as it caused me (I'm blaming the knob) to clip the curb.

I decided to go for a drive, which always gives me a great sense of freedom. I put on some tunes. Turned the volume up. Wound the window down. I braved the dynamic knob and let rip through the twisting country roads.

I drove to one of my favourite spots in the world – Staunton Harold. It's a converted stable yard with lots of artisan shops.

I browsed. I had coffee. I stood in the garden centre shed, absorbed the sweet, damp compost aroma; listened to the rain on the tin roof. I then popped to M & S and got myself a prepared sandwich, smoothie and yoghurt pot.

I can be shallow. I like a luxury. Cars have been my weakness since my black Ford Fiesta XR2. I love nature. That's my bliss. (We're back to Chapter 4 and what's important to you).

I grounded myself by re-seeing my life as if I was seeing it for the first time. I do the same thing with my daughter and husband. I study their faces. I look into their eyes. I observe them from a distance when they're not looking. I admire them.

ACTION:

- How can you re-see your work-life?
- How can you re-see your loved ones?
- How can you re-see yourself? I hate to harp on about it...but with all your gifts, talents, great traits and achievements.
- To enhance gratitude, use your senses. What are you seeing, hearing, smelling, tasting and feeling in that positive context?

So, my husband and I are sat in the consultant's office. This time my 'dedicated cancer support nurse' is with us. The heat has been turned up. It felt serious. He uttered his diagnosis in what seemed like slow motion. He used the c-word. I heard my husband's sharp intake of breath, as he tensed behind me. I had the less common, crappy kind of skin cancer – melanoma. Melanomas are more likely to metastasize from the skin to other organs than basal and squamous cell skin cancers and if they do, are more difficult to treat. Thoughts of a dear friend who lost her battle to skin cancer filled my mind.

I managed to hold it together until we were taken off to another room by the nurse to help process our feelings about it.

I cried again. Then she said the most wonderful thing, 'I have a ladder of worry which helps me to explain how concerned I am about you right now. You are currently on the lowest rung of my worry ladder.' My Inner Captain reminded me of this, whenever I had a wobble throughout the treatment.

After our appointment, we wandered aimlessly around the hospital, like we'd both lost all sense of direction. At that moment I saw so many sick people – far sicker than me. Playing on the TV screens was the news about a recent hurricane. People had lost their lives, loved ones and homes. I realised how lucky I was. I felt grateful.

Two operations and 12 months later I was given the all-clear. What that experience taught me is that we humans have an amazing capacity to cope; to be resilient when the crap hits the fan. To be grateful.

The Inner Brilliance, Outer Shine Journal – Processing Thoughts

There's a difference between ruminating and processing. Ruminating is going over either an event which happened in the past or hasn't even happened yet! It's the broken record that plays in your head. Processing effectively, enables you to deal with an event, so that it can be put to bed. You can come to terms with what happened and can move on from it. Because, what is the use of dragging up issues that occurred 30 years or 30 days ago? How does it serve us? Is it useful or useless? Preserve any learning, let go of the emotion.

Ruminating steals the moment we have right now. Constantly moaning going on and on about a problem either in your head or discussing it with another person and not actively trying to solve it, is going to hinder you. We burden ourselves. We burden other people with the same old woes.

Of course, you're allowed to complain, that can help you to process. However, if you keep telling the same old story, you are only hurting yourself, (and your pained listeners) and we're back to Groundhog Day.

As you already know, past stubborn stuff can require a technique such as Havening or EFT, (coming up in the next chapter). With other issues, simply deciding to take action to resolve the problem is all it needs. Being the Captain. Feeling empowered. Taking charge.

I use journaling to process my thoughts and feelings, as do my clients in between coaching sessions. I have a good old rant if I need to. (This is when my husband is grateful of my journaling, I don't dump copious amounts of poison in his ear and upset him in the process too). You're allowed to curse if you like. It is your journal. 'Better out than in', (your journal) is one of my mottos. And the great news is that studies show it's good for you.

In a 2005 study writing about traumatic, stressful or emotional events for 15–20 minutes on 3–5 occasions resulted in improvements in both physical and psychological health.[50] In another study, journaling helped the body to heal physical wounds quicker.[51]

I share a template with my clients when they start journaling. This is to help embed their Inner Captain, but also to ensure they sufficiently process events as far as they can. It also slowly weans them off needing coaching. Once their Inner Captain is fully developed, they might only require a coaching session now and then. Below is a list of prompts, which you can use to structure your journaling. Following this list also brings together quite a few topics covered in this book too:

1. **Get all your negativity out of the way**. Tell it like it is. No filtering. You want the purest form of your thoughts.
2. **Is there a potential Havening Topic?** When we experience strong, persistent emotions, this can be a sign of a feeling being re-triggered from your childhood, e.g.

'I got angry in the team meeting because my boss *belittled* me by saying XYZ. I felt totally *humiliated* and couldn't sleep last night.'

If you can identify your earliest memory of feeling 'belittled' or 'humiliated', ideally age 0-7, you can use Self Havening to diminish the trigger. You can find my 2-minute Havening video here:
https://www.youtube.com/watch?v=Mr8TkgIUxYI

3. **Spot any limiting beliefs** in your language, e.g. 'I'm sure that I'm going to lose my job'. I like to use a highlighter to flag any limiting beliefs.

4. Where possible, **re-state as an alternative useful belief**, e.g. We're all entitled to make mistakes. (This would be said in the voice of my 'Cheerleader').

5. If necessary, **use a challenging question or humour**, e.g. 'Crystal ball been on overtime again? How do you know? What is the worst that could happen? Then what would you do? What's your Plan B?' Use your humorous character voice for this.

6. **Identify your desired positive outcome**. What are you trying to achieve concerning this issue? Sometimes we lose sight of what we're moving towards. What would good look like? For example, 'I intend to go into the meeting with a positive mindset and listen to what my boss has to say.'

7. **Learning and self-awareness – information for your Bridge**, e.g. 'I've realised that working in an open plan office and being interrupted repeatedly by Sharon, is causing me stress.'

8. **Action** – one of the things that transform a coaching conversation from a nice conversation to a useful one, is having reflected and considered your options concerning an issue, you decide what you are now going to do about it. Otherwise, we are stuck in Groundhog Day or denial,

e.g. 'When I want to concentrate, I'm either going to take myself off to a meeting room and / or let Sharon know that I need some quiet time.'

9. **Positive Thoughts.** Having reflected on the negative, time to refocus your attention on what's working. Where are you making progress (this is good for filling up your Treasure Trove) and what is going well in your work-life right now? For example, 'I didn't put a task that wasn't mine on my production line. I stayed quiet in the meeting and let someone else take it. That has saved me 2 hours of work.'

10. **Gratitude.** Close your entry for the day with the things you grateful for, e.g. 'My partner looked amazing earlier.'

ACTION:

- Include journaling in your daily self-care routine. Pick a time each day when you can spend a few minutes reflecting. If you have nothing to say, don't do it. Once you have embedded your Inner Captain, use your journal when you need it.

Affirming Instructions

I used to think that affirmations were 'New Age', 'Pollyannaish' nonsense. However, in the book *Rich Habits*, the author Thomas C Corley illustrates some of the most effective daily success habits of wealthy individuals, which included using positive affirmations.[52] Also, in a study where patients were taught to turn negative thoughts or worries into affirmations they regained confidence and self-control.[53] This encouraged me to give them a go and I was surprised by the great things that 'occurred' in my work-life as a result of them. You can use affirmations to:

- **Re-affirm aspirations, your vision or goals**, e.g. 'I am working towards living in our dream home / location' or 'I have a thriving internet business.'

- **Diminish bad habits, fears, concerns or worries** by replacing them with empowering statements, e.g. 'I have too many things to do' would become, 'I am taking charge of my responsibilities and prioritising accordingly.'

Using affirmations was one of the things that contributed to me writing this book. Every morning the year before I wrote this book, I would read, 'I am working towards being a published author'. It kicked me up the rear and forced me to think about it each day.

I tend to read my affirmations as part of my self-care regime after I have done my journaling in the morning. They are written on a note on my phone. I have used it for all sorts of habit change ranging from:

- Diet, exercise and health
- Family
- State of mind
- Personal development
- Fee income targets / money / business development
- Future / vision / goals

It takes 2 minutes to read each day. Can you spare 2 minutes for *project me time*?

Summary of Key Points:
- Your thinking is influencing your biology and the results you are getting in work-life.
- You are the custodian of your beliefs now – regardless of whether someone in your past 'caused' them. Don't be a victim, take charge and activate your Inner Captain.
- Remember that we can switch on the equivalent of

Blackpool Illuminations in our head. Catch the first lightbulb, and use one of these techniques: distraction, tell the thought to stop, EFT (next chapter) or Havening.

- When you find yourself 'What if-ing', to disarm the thought and reduce rumination, work out how you would cope if the worst did happen. What would your Plan B be?

- To develop your Bridge – your self-awareness; the extra 4% that most of the population don't use, notice whether what you are thinking is useful or use-less. If it is hindering, use one of the Blackpool Illumination strategies mentioned above.

- We all have off days. Bad moods come and go. Be safe in the knowledge that states rise and fall all the time. We don't laugh at jokes forever. Therefore, don't automatically assume you are depressed. If you apply the strategies in this book, you are more likely to avoid depression altogether – except for when your body and mind need it, for example when you are grieving or have experienced loss.

- Re-see your life. Avoid re-dipping the bad bits. Recognise what is great. It'll do you good.

- Use *The Inner Brilliance, Outer Shine Journal* to embed your Inner Captain thoughts and to offload and process negative emotions.

- Keep yourself on track to Destination Joy through your affirmations.

- Finally, don't let negative thoughts about yesterday or tomorrow, steal your presence of today.

Chapter 9

Antidote #9: Learn to Handle Rough Seas

It's not what you do, but the state you do it in.
The Optimum Health Clinic

Our state of mind is our way of being at any moment. State of mind becomes important if we work on the premise that it influences our decisions, (I once bought a midlife crisis impractical sports car, only to sell it 3 weeks later and lose thousands of pounds, because I was in a strange mood when I purchased it), behaviour, action or inaction, and ultimately our performance and the results we get. We damage our state of mind when we overwork or bash ourselves with a metaphoric imposter syndrome stick. Our state of mind also influences how much we shine too. It becomes self-perpetuating. The happier we feel the more we shine. The more we shine the more people and natural success is drawn towards us.

In every moment of every day, we get to choose whether we enhance our shine; how we navigate away from the rocks and handle the rough seas – you do have that power, as hopefully, you will see in this chapter.

Boosting Performance

Recently I had coffee with an old client, who has become a friend. She was the one who kicked me up the rear to get on and write this book. She is the one who encouraged me to achieve another life-long ambition to ski. Our conversation turned to the French Alps. A few years ago, her performance dropped off whilst her friends' skiing had improved, so she decided to have a top-up lesson to get her back on track.

Her ski instructor – 'the lovely Tom' took her down the

kiddies' penguin slope to begin with. She had to do a variety of mini jumps and duck under arches. Then they went off-piste for an hour and she had to ski on knee-deep snow. It drove her mad and she felt frustrated.

Tom sensed this and asked her how she felt when she'd finished a challenging run in the past. This was clever. She started to recall a time when her performance was at its best and re-played this in her mind's eye. Re-seeing the positive movie triggered good feelings – she was re-dipping in a good way! He asked her how she felt now, and she said, 'I feel great!' Her face lit up as her feelings shifted from frustrated to excited. She set off on the red run which they'd just approached, without a second thought.

What Tom did was get her to access the state of mind she needed to take on the red run; he helped her to change state.

ACTION:

Experiment changing your state right now:

- First identify how you currently feel, e.g. neutral, frustrated, stressed
- Next, identify the alternative state of mind you would like instead, e.g. calm, tranquil, happy
- Now go back to a time in the past when you felt your desired state of mind
- Then really, see it, hear it and feel it
- Repeat until you have a good waft of those feelings

What did you notice? Our minds are malleable, and we can take charge. The hardest part is recognising when we need to take charge – using our Bridge. i.e. being tuned in to all the information we are receiving in our mind and the sensations in our body. Then passing this information onto the Captain to re-direct your vessel away from the rocks. In every moment of every day, we get to choose whether we make it a good or a bad moment. We can 'choose' by influencing our state by the strategies that follow in this chapter.

State of Mind

State of mind is a culmination of:

- What we think
- What we feel
- How we use and hold our body
- Neurochemicals and hormones

For example, when we observe someone watching a TV sketch which they think is funny their body may move back and forth whilst they laugh. As they laugh, they will release the neuropeptide endorphin which relieves pain and produces feelings of euphoria and pleasure.

Conversely, when you see someone in a depressed state, for example, following a relationship breakdown, you may notice that they hold their body in a slumped or closed posture as the person thinks or talks about the relationship, which triggers feelings of sadness. Repeating this cycle of thinking (ruminating) then embeds the depressed state. When we are depressed the neurotransmitters serotonin, norepinephrine, and dopamine are involved.

We can change our state by using our Bridge to first recognise what is going on and then engaging our Captain to redirect our state, by taking constructive action. We can change:

1. **How we think** – see Chapter 8. Every thought we have causes neurochemical changes. For example, practising gratitude produces dopamine and serotonin, two neurotransmitters which are responsible for happiness and contentment.[54]

2. **How we feel** – we create meta feelings about feelings our bodies have just experienced. An example of this would be feeling annoyed with yourself following an angry outburst in a team meeting. We'll look at how you can circumnavigate these feelings later.

3. **Our neurochemicals and hormones** by taking charge of what we think, feel and do. We can influence our biology too. For example, what exercise we take and the food we consume, (more about these things in Chapter 10) or choosing to perk yourself up, having recognised that you're in a negative state by spending time with someone who makes you laugh.

In essence, everything is inextricably linked. Our state of mind is an expression of what's happening on the inside. This is expressed through our non-verbal communication on the outside and influences how much we shine. Our state of mind also affects our performance at work. The great news is that our Captain can take charge of this and create more positive and effective states of mind.

Why State Matters:

In a study of 740 leaders conducted by Alexander Caillet, Jeremy Hirshberg and Stefano Petti, they selected 18 states of mind and asked the leaders how often they experienced them and what impact it had on their effectiveness and performance.

They identified, '94% of respondents reported that Calm, Happy and Energized (CHE) are the three that drive the greatest levels of effectiveness and performance. However, Frustrated, Anxious, Tired and Stressed (FATS) states of mind were also relatively common. Most leaders reported that FATS states often yield benefits in the short term but are detrimental in the long term – especially to relationships.'[55]

States vary in intensity and length, for example when

someone tells you a joke, you may laugh hard until you are crying and keep laughing for several minutes as you replay the joke in your head or giggle for a few seconds. That would be a good use of your Captain!

Equally, have you noticed how much energy you expend, having had an emotional outburst or spent time with someone who was intensely emotional? How drained you can feel once the intense emotion dissipates? More about how to gain more energy in the final chapter.

When State Damages Our Performance

My thinking and performance were disrupted recently at my grandad's funeral when I was asked to share a reading that was important to him. Not only were the words very moving, but for obvious reasons, other feelings were going on too. I found it really tough. All I had to do was read from a script. I didn't have to remember a thing. So what went wrong?

My performance was poor and it caught me by surprise. My Captain had gone AWOL because *I'd been a public speaker for 25 years*. The sheer arrogance of it, ay? I didn't think I needed to manage my state and to be honest, I'd clocked off. I was wrapped up in seeing my grandad's smiling face in his cowboy hat on the order of service, followed by his coffin being carried down the church aisle. It triggered a variety of different and unexpected feelings.

I had no time to process them and so tried to push them beneath the surface. Big mistake.

Susan David, a Harvard School Medical psychologist in her book, *Emotional Agility: Get Unstuck, Embrace Change, and Thrive in Work and Life*, refers to 'bottlers'. These are people that bottle up their feelings and she says, 'Unfortunately, trying not to do something takes a surprising amount of mental bandwidth. And research shows that attempting to minimise or ignore thoughts and emotions only serves to amplify them'.[56]

If you do one thing, admit how you are feeling. Acknowledging will start to help to dissipate the thought or feeling. Your unconscious mind has given you the thought / feeling and is wanting your attention. So, let your Autopilot know you have heard them. For example, using your Inner Captain you could say to yourself, 'I am angry/sad/frustrated/nervous etc. about X and that's OK. Feelings are normal.' When you learn EFT later in this chapter, you will be able to shift feelings with gusto!

Unprocessed, bottled, unadmitted feelings have a way of making an appearance; a way of making themselves heard. It was my turn to approach the lectern.

For the first 30 seconds of the reading, my voice sounded like a cross between a pre-pubescent teenager, Tarzan and a horse race commentator. I couldn't look at my audience. I had sweaty palms and was scared that I was going to cry. I had to quickly wake my Captain up and take charge of my state. I took a breath (more about breathing later), slowed the pace of my voice and adjusted my body.

After the funeral, I went to speak to my cousin; he'd found it tough too – also a veteran public speaker. The emotional component knocked me off course, which interfered with my performance.

Rocks and Rough Seas

I was at the races with my friends and one of them turned to me and said with sad puppy dog eyes, 'And how are you? You've had a tough time haven't you?' My kind sweet friend. Always empathetic and concerned for people.

At first, I thought the question was being directed at someone else and began to turn around to see if it was one of my other friends in her line of sight. Realising she was talking to me, I got with the program, rewound the tape for last 12-18 months, (I didn't want to break rapport by immediately disagreeing with her), and said, 'Errrrm yes, there have been tough spots, but errrrm it actually feels like it has been a great year.' I broke rapport. I've never been good at telling a porky. My friend was also right, there had been some tough times.

I wish I had a magic wand to wipe away all the crappy events we have to deal with in life. The sad fact of the matter is that the waters will get rough at times, but what I've learnt over the years is that the more self-development work you do, (by using the strategies I share in this book), the more resilient you can become.

Your inner dialogue becomes less critical because limiting beliefs have been dissolved, through Havening, EFT and taking positive action. Those critical voices were never yours anyway, (they're often someone else's from our past)! Unhelpful behaviours and emotions recur less. You can deal with more and it takes you longer to reach full capacity from a stress point of view. Aches, pains and illnesses magically disappear. Ultimately your Ship is light and agile enough to be able to better navigate through the rough seas.

The reason I felt confused when my friend said I'd had a tough year, is that I had processed those experiences, (you are going to learn how to use another tool which will help you to process unhelpful emotions in this chapter). It was difficult at the time, but those incidents hadn't tarnished my whole year. From my perspective, we'd been to three wonderful weddings, had the ski-trip of a lifetime with my stepson and daughter-in-law, I'd written this book and business was booming. Those were the experiences that left a lasting imprint on my year. The other incidents had been dissolved.

We are feeling beings. Our feelings give our life meaning. Is our work-life good or not so good? Our emotions set us into motion. Our feelings contribute to whether we shine or not. Throughout this book I have used the terms feeling and emotion interchangeably, to mean the same thing. We are now going to dig deeper into emotions and their origins.

Joy Has Competition

Let's work on the basis that you want more joy in your work-life and you have identified a vision and plan of how you're going to get there. However, as demonstrated above, we can come across rocks and rough seas. Depending on which theory you read, joy has competition, because there are seven other emotions which we can experience.

There are lots of different theories about emotions and there is currently no consensus on a definition, with estimates ranging from four through to 34,000 different ones. However, Robert Plutchik an American Psychologist identified eight primary emotions that serve as the foundation for all others. He built a visual tool called The Wheel of Emotions and listed them as contrasting polar pairs: anger vs fear, joy vs sadness, trust vs disgust and surprise vs anticipation.[57]

Joy has even more competition when we allow imposter thoughts and overwork as a result of them. There is no headspace for us to experience joy – particularly when our personal / free time has been squeezed to the minimum to accommodate work.

Emotions are hardwired, innate and universal. They are physical and instinctive. Emotions come from the limbic system and have helped us survive. The limbic system is located deep within the brain and is responsible for behavioural and emotional responses. We experience emotions in our body and their purpose is to automatically trigger a response to a stimulus.

For example, when someone cuts you up on your way to work, you don't think, 'Ooo time to stop', you slam on your brakes instinctively so that you don't go into the back of the other vehicle. You feel a physical jolt in your body and your muscles tense; your breath and pulse quicken. Once the threat has passed your body returns to normal. That's how emotions should work. However, we can wind ourselves up and create a negative state of mind (which encompasses feelings, body tension or shape, neurochemicals and hormones) because of what we think about the said event.

In Viktor Frankl's book, *Man's Search for Meaning: The classic tribute to hope from the Holocaust,* he says, 'Between stimulus and response there is a space. In that space is our power to choose our response. In our response lies our growth and our freedom.' Our opportunity lies in how we react and deal with our feelings, for example, our feelings, about feelings.

Meta Emotions

Meta-emotion is 'an organized and structured set of emotions and cognitions about the emotions, both one's own emotions and the emotions of others.'[58] So, in other words, we have feelings about our feelings or other people's feelings. There are four types of meta-emotions:

1. **Negative-negative**, e.g. feeling remorse about feeling angry having shouted at the driver who cut you up.
2. **Negative-positive,** e.g. feeling guilty about feeling generally happy, having spent time with someone who was down on their luck.
3. **Positive-positive,** e.g. feeling happy about someone else's joy, having passed an exam.
4. **Positive-negative,** e.g. feeling glad about feeling angry following an emotional outburst in a meeting.

In a study by the Greater Good Science Center based at UC Berkeley, they found that **people who had more frequent negative-negative meta-emotions also experienced greater feelings of depression and that it wasn't associated with any other types of meta emotion.** They discovered that many people get upset, nervous, or angry about their own negative emotions, in particular.[59]

ACTION:

- What meta emotions have occurred lately?
- Which of the four types of meta emotion do you generally experience?
- What are you going to choose to do differently?

We have the power to choose, how we deal with our emotions and thinking, hence the previous chapter. Your Captain is in charge of managing the space between stimulus and response. Remember that we can operate up to 5%, more consciously, with your Autopilot taking care of the remaining 95%. However, your average human being will run on Autopilot 99% of the time.

For example, if following a tense exchange in a meeting with a colleague who addressed the fact you'd not delivered on an objective, (which resulted in you feeling shame), and then when you return to your desk, you chunter to yourself about the incident, which triggers the meta feeling anger – you are responsible for that feeling. Not anyone else.

Are you going to lengthen the period you hurt yourself – and potentially other people? Think about how things can snowball sometimes, because of one incident. Or are you going to use your Bridge to tune into what you are thinking, feeling and how you are behaving and get your Captain to re-direct your Ship back towards Destination Joy?

You could simply choose to take a deep relaxing breath, (more about this in the next chapter), which would put the break on your fight or flight system and accelerate your parasympathetic nervous system, which helps to calm you down. Or you could take yourself off to the loos and do some tapping, which is what's coming up next!

When Your Bucket is Overflowing

One of the analogies I use to explain state is the bucket. The more negative triggers you experience throughout the day, the higher the water level becomes, the greater the risk of you overflowing emotionally and behaviourally.

For example, you get up, having tossed and turned the night before because of a project you are concerned about at work. You're already tired and the day has only just begun! You check in on your mail and you've got an email from that obnoxious work colleague. You pen a quick flamer back and triumphantly press send.

Because you're tired, you trip up over the dog which causes you to spill your coffee. You're already late as you hit the snooze button three times and haven't got time for cleaning up! You shove a processed sugar fuelled cereal bar down your throat for speed, which creates a mini energy high and then a grumpy slump.

You go to your wardrobe and realise you are out of shirts and have to put on yesterday's crinkly, smelly one. Then you reach the motorway and there's an accident. You have to bump your 9 am appointment. As you're sat in the traffic jam, you start to reflect on what you said in your flame-mail and wonder if you were quick to temper. You worry about facing your colleague. You've not even got to work yet, and your bucket is overflowing.

How can we perform at our best when we are in that kind of state? Most of the things that occurred above are within our control.

Under Captain's Orders

Our lack of sleep creates a chain reaction of events, which other than the traffic jam, are within our control – even then there are apps which we can use to send us notifications of any traffic issues so that we can take an alternative route.

We need to be alert to the information coming in on our Bridge. If the night before, we'd realised that we were concerned about the project, what we could have done is use *The Inner Brilliance, Outer Shine Journal* to process what we actually think about the project to allay any worries, as opposed to ruminating and tossing and turning. We could have made ourselves feel like the Captain by identifying what is within our power and control and identifying a 'Plan B'. We could have calmed ourselves with our reassuring and compassionate Inner Captain, (I'd use my 'Cheerleader' for this).

We could have done some yoga to release the tension of the day from our bodies and calm our fight or flight system so that we were able to drift off to sleep more soundly and stay asleep.

When we wake up in the middle of the night, (often having crashed through exhaustion), it can be because we've not processed enough information during the day. Therefore, this build-up of thoughts must be dealt with during 'night shift' whilst we are in dream sleep. Giving our brain too many things to sort out, can then cause our system to crash and wake up.

If I feel overloaded before I sleep or wake up in the middle of the night, I empty my brain by writing everything down. That way, my mind can relax and get on with sleeping. I will be going into why sleep is so important for us physiologically and how to get more of it, in the next chapter.

Calming Rough Waters: EFT (Emotional Freedom Technique)

Throw a pebble in the water and it will create ripples. Throw a boulder and it will make waves. Throw a series of boulders and it takes a while for the waters to calm.

If you're impatient like me and you want to circumnavigate this process and are keen to make a quicker recovery from something that has created ripples, waves or your bucket to overflow, you can use EFT. Emotions can catch us unawares. I've used EFT en route to business meetings a few times. Feeling the flip of my stomach and the slight buzz of anxiety before pitching for a piece of work is unhelpful, so I tap (use EFT) the feelings away.

Equally, sometimes we have a hell of a day. We are lost at

sea with our emotions and feel overwhelmed by the build-up of negative triggers throughout the day. EFT was my go-to tool before I discovered Havening. It's not as straight forward as Havening, which is probably why I use it less but can be as effective. Havening was designed having researched the effectiveness of TFT (Thought Field Therapy) which was the forerunner to EFT.

For example, I once got a message as I was about to go to bed. I went from 0-60 in 1 second. My face was bright red. All my sleepiness dissipated in an instant. I told my husband briefly what had happened and explained that I knew I wouldn't sleep unless I sorted myself out. I went downstairs to my study and journaled – that didn't do it. It moved the issue on and helped me to gain clarity, but I still felt wound up, so used EFT to shift it. Within 20 minutes the whole issue was put to bed and I slept like a baby.

ACTION:
- When have emotions caught you off guard?
- When have you felt overwhelmed by emotions, to the extent where it impacted your performance?
- Which emotional states would you like to be able to shift?

What is EFT?

EFT releases emotional blockages in your energy system by tapping on acupressure points on the body. EFT is based on the same energy meridians used in traditional acupuncture to treat physical and emotional ailments for over 5,000 years but without needles.

Now, if you're as sceptical as I was when I first came across 'tapping' that's OK. Like Havening, you've got to experience it to believe it. Also, you must experience it in the right way, because whatever you happen to be thinking of at the time as you tap – is what you'll be working on.

When I first set up my business 15 years ago, I would get up at 5 am three mornings a week to network. A fellow networker introduced my associates and me to tapping. Not only did he invade my personal space by tapping various points on my body – he did it in public. I felt so embarrassed.

Anyway, he said various things which I had to repeat, whilst he tapped away on me like a woodpecker and then declared I was 'cured'. All I could think was, *I feel like a right idiot doing this in front of everyone*. Feeling like an idiot became the issue I worked on (because EFT works on whatever you are thinking). I just didn't realise it at the time.

I then avoided the technique like the plague for 6 years declaring that it was a load of old rubbish and didn't work, because the thing he was supposedly changing hadn't been 'cured'. I later learnt when I eventually trained as an EFT Practitioner that this was because I was thinking about something else. When you use EFT it is like editing a document; you could have lots of them open in Word, but unless it is onscreen as you tap on your keyboard, the document won't get modified – so no thinking about what you're having for your tea as you tap on each point later!

Then I got diagnosed with ME I signed up to The Optimum Health Clinic and as part of their programme, was assigned an EFTer. He changed my life. Such a kind, compassionate and clever being – he could see right through me and could always get to the root cause of an emotional issue. Whilst ME is a biological disease, we increase our toxic load and exacerbate the illness, through our toxic thoughts – and I had a few! Hence the need for a journal. We can raise our awareness of what those toxic thoughts are and then tap on them if needs be.

EFT Efficacy

Researcher Dr. Dawson Church, Ph.D., founder of the National Institute for Integrative Healthcare analysed the results of over 40 EFT studies. He's identified that EFT is effective for a wide range of emotional problems, including:

- Performance
- Phobias
- Pain
- Anxiety
- Depression
- PTSD (Post Traumatic Stress Disorder)
- Weight loss and food[60]

Dr. Mercola is an alternative medicine advocate, osteopathic physician and bestselling author. On his website, he quotes many EFT studies saying, 'Recent research found that, compared to the control group, it significantly increased positive emotions, such as hope and enjoyment, and decreased negative emotional states like anger and shame'.[61]

The bottom line is that using EFT is going to enhance the power of your Captain, by equipping you with another tool which can diminish your negative emotions and help you to redirect your Ship towards Destination Joy, whenever you feel yourself drifting in the direction of Destination Grim.

How to Use EFT

When using EFT, the first step is to identify the problem. This could be a thought, feeling or sensation in your body. We call this the problem statement.

Using EFT requires you to tap on various meridian points whilst using a reminder phrase to keep you focused on the problem statement.

I tend to use EFT to shift in the moment states, such as having had a bad day (and my bucket is overflowing) or being triggered unexpectedly by something. You can however use it for specific events in the same way you use Havening.

For the purposes of this book, we're going to use EFT to shift states – get rid of them. Calm the waters. Relax your system, so that you can go about your business without feeling overloaded or disrupted by your emotions.

I also use EFT when there is a persistent limiting belief, or the client is sceptical about their change. For example, the Havening work is complete, but because the client hasn't been fully 'tested' i.e. been back in the context which triggered them in the first place, they don't believe anything is different.

I once treated a client who used to panic on planes and on their first trip abroad following their session, (so this was a real test of whether the Havening had worked), had zero panic symptoms but continued to put this down to other factors. Their physiological signs had changed – they were no longer being triggered; it was their belief system which needed updating using EFT.

Using EFT is like playing pass the parcel; there can be many layers, but if you keep going you'll get to the prize. You might start tapping on one problem statement, such as, 'I feel really pissed off with Judy because she dismissed my idea in a meeting today'. You would then use the reminder phrase: 'Pissed off with Judy' to stay focussed and ensure you're 'editing' the right document. This would be your first round of EFT – your first layer.

Having tapped on being pissed off with Judy, you might then think, 'The reason I was pissed off with Judy, was because she embarrassed me in front of all my peers'. This would become your second problem statement. You could use the reminder phrase: 'embarrassed in front of my peers'. Layer number two.

As you're tapping on that problem statement, a memory might pop into your head of other times in the past when you have felt embarrassed in front of your peers. You will be inadvertently working on all these memories as you think of them. You may want to do several rounds of tapping (I'll explain what a round of tapping is in a moment) on all these memories until they feel neutralised and 0/10 in terms of feelings. This is the gift of EFT; you've defused the nasty feelings. You can use the same scoring system we used with Havening. Ten being the strongest negative feeling, zero being no feeling – neutralised.

Alternatively, you could revert to using Havening once you've identified the memories. I often use EFT to get clients to tune into memories connected to their language and then finish the events off with Havening. If you're unsure of what you really think or feel, write it out in your journal, then use EFT on the language in your sentences.

You keep tapping and unpeeling the layers until you get to the prize, which is often a neutral state. This is a sign that the state has been neutralised and has shifted. For me, that's boredom or nothingness – no thoughts or feelings.

Now, unless you get to the earliest or most traumatic childhood memory either using EFT or Havening, 'feeling embarrassed in front of peers' will recur. However, what you will have done using EFT is shifted your state at that moment, so that you can resume normal service.

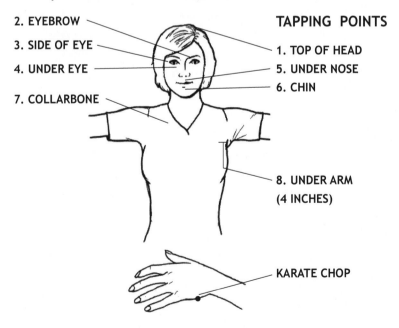

TAPPING POINTS

2. EYEBROW
3. SIDE OF EYE
4. UNDER EYE
7. COLLARBONE

1. TOP OF HEAD
5. UNDER NOSE
6. CHIN

8. UNDER ARM (4 INCHES)

KARATE CHOP

EFT instructions:

1. Identify the problem statement which can be a thought, feeling or sensation in your body, e.g. my stomach is churning.

2. Score the intensity of this statement out of 10. Ten being the strongest negative feeling, 0 being no feeling, i.e. it has been neutralised.

3. Tap on the karate chop point with two fingers and repeat this statement three times: 'Even though [insert problem statement e.g. I feel really pissed off with Judy because she dismissed my idea in a meeting today] I love and accept myself anyway.' If saying you love yourself is a step too far – as it can be for some clients, simply say 'I accept myself anyway.'

4. Then use your reminder phrase, e.g. 'Pissed off with Judy' to tap on all other points about seven times in the order shown on the diagram.

5. Once you've completed one round, i.e. tapped on all points, you can either rescore the intensity of your original problem statement and carry out repeat rounds until the score goes to zero, or unpeel the next layer of the parcel and tap on the related thought or feeling that comes up.

6. Carry on until you are bored and the original state has been neutralised.

I worked with two EFT practitioners for months. Bit by bit, we chipped away at limiting beliefs, behaviours and emotions using EFT and I started to recover. I went from not having enough energy to climb the stairs to being able to hop up a mountain and ski!

ACTION:

- Review *The Inner Brilliance, Outer Shine Journal* and see if you can spot any toxic thoughts or feelings. Then tap on them.

- Alternatively, tap on something that is currently weighing you down and creating emotional ripples.

Cultivating Joy

So, having learnt how to handle rough seas and get rid of the things that elbow joy out of the way, it's important to consciously create opportunities to cultivate more of it. Originally, when I started contemplating my 'joyful' experiences, my mind took me back to when I was a little girl. I had very few reference points as an adult.

When I was 10 and my sister was 7, we'd get dropped off at one of Morecambe's top attractions: The Fun House. It was like soft play only for hard nuts. Girls dressed in ra-ra skirts would proudly display second-degree burns from the vertical slide as a badge of honour. Sometimes my Dad and his girlfriend would join us.

One of our favourite activities was a six-foot-wide wooden tunnel, which rotated. If you sat in it, you'd move up the rotating wall and then slip down again. My Dad would take things to the next level and stand spread-eagled and hang on for a full rotation – like he was doing a cartwheel. My sister and I would stand there mouths agog, quickly turning around to check out whether any of the other kids were watching and to see if they were impressed or not. On subsequent visits, he was encouraged to repeat his trick. He knew how to have fun.

I have eluded to the fact that I can be Miss Stiff Knickers. My first realisation of needing to lighten up was when my daughter was 4. We'd gone away for a weekend break with my extended family. It was fantastic. Just like the good old days when we'd all gather for prawn cocktail and roast beef dinner at my Nana and Grandad's house on a Sunday.

We'd rented a big house in Penrith, and it was January. Probably not the best time of year to head north but my Nana was treating us all for her birthday. On our journey to the house, snow started to hit the windscreen in a hypnotic swathe, to the extent where we considered turning back. When we eventually arrived it was late, so we went straight to bed.

When we got up, we did a tour of the hilly gardens which were covered in snow. The owners had thoughtfully left us a sledge! I joined forces with my cousins, and we set about building a snowman for my daughter. Then we all regressed. My daughter wasn't too keen on trying out the sledge, so my cousin and I decided to carry out a demonstration. We flew down the hill laughing and screaming (in a good way).

The look of disgust on my daughter's face. She stood stomping at the top of the hill, with her hands on her hips and shouted, 'Calm down Mummy. You're not supposed to have fun!' That was when I realised I wasn't having nearly enough fun in life. Me having fun was an alien and unnerving concept to her.

ACTION:

- What do you love doing?
- What makes you go weeeee in your head / aloud?
- When was the last time you did something like that?
- When can you do it again?

Scheduling Joy

Research has shown that for many, the positive effect of anticipating their holiday will be stronger than the actual event and happiness will increase in the period before your holiday but be less afterwards.[62] This makes sense. How many times have you indulged yourself imagining what a holiday will be like – especially when it's dark, cold and miserable? Equally, how do you feel when you return?

We schedule joy with our best mates, Bob, Ju and Jess too. We are guaranteed belly laughs when we are with them. Ju laughs like Muttley from Wacky Races and sees the funny side in most everyday situations. Bob, who initially when you first meet him seems quiet and shy, will spontaneously dance like a puppet with imaginary strings on his hands and feet and sing like Elvis when you least expect it. Jess is one of the sweetest girls I know.

One of the memories we have lived off for years and re-laughed at many times was when we went to the Cotswolds for the weekend. Typical of our group, we tend to get over-excited and peak too soon on the first night. We'd managed to polish off a bottle of red wine before dinner – so empty stomachs.

When we eventually arrived at the restaurant with our red wine-stained lips, the waitress was snooty with us, (I think I would be standoffish if I saw us wandering in). Anyway, somebody cracks a joke (not about the waitress) as she was handing out the menus and I spluttered a little. Trying to recover quickly and feeling embarrassed I said, 'Did aaaa spray yerrr?'

We must learn to stop the wheel, to slow time and access the joy of life. We must discipline ourselves by scheduling time to live life in the space in between work.

That's the great thing about joy-filled memories; they're yours forever and you can re-dip into them any time. Therefore, how about scheduling more joy?

ACTION:

- What brings you joy? Examples could include, sporting activities such as horse riding, skiing, going for a walk, weekends away, camping, visiting historic buildings, having friends around for dinner, booking a series of classes, baking, reading, painting, going to concerts, listening to music, having an uninterrupted cup of herbal tea etc.
- What else could you book in your diary that will bring you joy? I like to have at least one thing in a week – I don't tend to schedule a cuppa, but each to their own.

- What or whom steals your joy? What do you need to be doing less of? This could be cleaning, (I prefer to have fewer handbags and gain the time back), maintaining a one-way friendship or clutter, etc.

Summary of Key Points:
- States of mind are a culmination of what we think feel and how we hold our body, which then produces neurochemicals and hormones. We can be the Captain and either create an upward positive spiral of emotions, or a downward spiral. Using your Bridge to monitor incoming information and then passing this onto your Captain to redirect your Ship, helps you to access more joyful and productive states of mind.
- You can change your state by changing your thinking, your feelings (using EFT or Havening), and how you move your body. This will trigger a more positive concoction of chemicals inside.
- There will always be rocks and rough seas; it's how we choose to deal with them that counts. The more Havening and EFT work you do, the more buoyancy you will have, the easier it will be to redirect your Ship back towards Destination Joy.
- Recognise when you are creating feelings about feelings. Remember there is space between the original trigger and your reaction. Redirect your response using one of your Inner Captain's voices, take a breath, distract yourself, journal, use EFT or Havening. You have so many tools at your disposal now.
- Get yourself back on-line, performing, focusing, whatever the state is that you need at that moment, by dissipating negative states using EFT.
- Give joy a chance. Identify what you love to do, re-fun your life and schedule some joy-inducing activities.

Chapter 10

Antidote #10: Access the Mess Deck

Time And health are two precious assets that we don't recognize and appreciate until they have been depleted.
Denis Waitley

We are in the Mess Deck of your Ship. The mess deck is traditionally the place where sailors would rest, relax, re-fuel, and re-charge. What follows are the good habits which will counterbalance any remaining bad imposter syndrome, workaholic habits. They will help you stay physically healthy, full of energy and will polish off your shine. Because, if we don't take care of our body, work and life can become very difficult if we are tired, exhausted, in pain or sick – there isn't any time for joy!

My Manifesto for Your Change
It would be easy to skip this final chapter thinking it doesn't apply to you, as I did many years ago. To deny change was necessary. To stay stuck in Groundhog Day, putting up with my symptoms, hoping they would magically disappear. All I did was delay my recovery. And yet sometimes, we treat ourselves as though we are an invincible machine that can power on through regardless, without the same care, attention and nurture given to children, to ensure they survive and flourish.

We put ourselves on the backburner. We eat nutritionally deficient convenience food to save ourselves time and effort. But why? So that we have more time to work? We pop pills to mask any pain, as opposed to understanding what our body is trying to tell us. We fail to get to the root cause. We skimp on sleep.

But what happens to our Ship if we put the wrong fuel in, fail to rest our crew or make inadequate harbour stops for servicing, repair and maintenance?

Do you remember my client Charlotte at the very start of this book? An executive in both work and life. She said the real reason she came to see me was that she wanted to be able to see her kids grow up. She wanted to stop being sick, consumed by her thoughts and so busy that she'd miss what was happening in front of her own eyes.

She felt dissociated from her family life and was going through the motions. She couldn't travel anywhere without taking her medicine cabinet with her. There was no room for joy and when she did participate in activities that were meant to be joy-fuelled; she was so locked in her head, analysing what may or may not happen and tuned into her physiological symptoms that she missed the moment.

She was plagued by irritable bowel syndrome (IBS), heartburn and arthritic pain. Life was happening to her, like some script playing out, as opposed to her being in, what she was in.

How can we enjoy life when we are distracted by our thoughts, feelings (hence the previous chapters) and poor health?

Missing Life and Making Ourselves Sick

One of my favourite films is *Click*, which is a 2006 American science fantasy comedy film directed by Frank Coraci, written by Steve Koren and Mark O'Keefe, and produced by Adam Sandler, who also stars in the lead role. Not only is this movie really funny, but as with many of Adam Sandler's movies, if you look below the surface of all his buffooning, there is a deep psychological message.

Adam Sandler is an executive, wanting to become a partner in an architect's firm. He keeps being given false hope by his boss David Hasselhoff, that if he gets the latest project over the line, he will make partner. Sandler works long hours, eats a lot of Twinkies and cancels family holidays to get partnership. His boss continues to move the goalposts.

The science fantasy part of the film is a remote control for his life, which he is gifted in a DIY store. He can fast forward through anything that stops him from working, such as family dinners, making love to his wife, illness and playing with his kids. In the end, the remote control goes on autopilot, so that he always fast-forwards through these things, until he eventually arrives at his deathbed.

His father has died. He rewinds to the last time he saw his Dad and watches the scene over and over. He feels deep sadness, shame and regrets his behaviour – he was there with him, but not present with him. His kids have grown up and become distant, his wife has re-married the speedo wearing swimming instructor...but he is the CEO of a huge firm! He's got massively overweight, had lots of illnesses and is now dying prematurely because he's worked so hard.

This movie always makes me tear up because it is like some of the stories I hear from my clients and is always a good kick up the bum for yours truly. My clients talk about being on a hamster wheel that never stops – even on holiday. What about taking a mini-holiday every day? More about this later. For now, let's focus on how you prevent yourself from being sick or exhausted so that you are fit and able to enjoy yourself in the first place.

ACTION:

What are you like when you are sick, tired, exhausted or in pain? What's the impact on:

- Your performance at work?
- Your relationships at work?
- The relationships in your personal life?
- What you eat?

- How you exercise?
- How you spend your leisure time?

Your Energy Bank

When I was diagnosed with ME I was referred to a specialised NHS clinic. One of the things that stuck with me was their 'Energy Bank' analogy, not just for personal use, but for my clients. When you have ME you are taught to pace your use of energy. People who get ME tend to be high achiever types, who are constantly on the go – hence the need for pacing. They operate as if they have long-life Duracell batteries.

ME was initially referred to as 'Yuppie flu' because it seemed to affect young, middle-class professionals. I can remember seeing images on the news of Porsche driving stockbrokers, drinking champagne on the Canary Wharf. They were burning the candle at both ends – like my client Charlotte.

The nurse at the ME clinic asked me to think about my energy use being like a bank. You can make deposits and withdrawals. If you make too many withdrawals, you will go bankrupt, (get sick or exhausted). She asked me to think about what constituted as good energy deposits and what withdrew my energy.

Examples of good energy deposits include:

- **The quality of the fuel we put in our bodies.** Ever put cheap fuel in your car and noticed how it splutters? We are not too dissimilar. More about this later. Charlotte admitted that she was drinking every night either to unwind or whilst entertaining clients. She slipped into conversation that she 'only drank two bottles of wine the other night' whilst doing business.
- **The quality of our sleep** - in Tom Rath's book, *Eat Move Sleep: How Small Choices Lead to Big Changes* he says that if you are going to prioritise anything, prioritise your sleep because if you're tired the next day, it influences what

you eat and what you eat influences how much exercise you take.[63]

- **How we use our bodies** – doing the right amount of exercise. Do nothing at all is lethal as is over-exercising because it can cause inflammation, which is linked to chronic diseases such as cancer, heart disease, dementia and diabetes. In a study of elite adolescent male and female basketball players, inflammatory markers spiked following a single exercise as well as exercise training.[64] Yay I hear you say. Don't go cancelling your gym membership just yet.

- **Making time for rest and play so that we recover from stress** – for example, having fun and carrying out activities that bring you joy, spending time with radiators, as opposed to drains as referred to in Chapter 2, learning to relax your body and mind every day so that you stay in optimum health and socialising – although not too much (killjoy) as that can take it out of you too!

I'm going to cover how you can make great energy deposits in this chapter.

When it comes to going overdrawn at the energy bank, every single action requires an energy withdrawal, whether that is beating your heart or holding an emotionally charged conversation.

When we make excessive energy withdrawals, this is when we get into trouble and our body and state of mind start to creak. For example, poor quality sleep the night before will cause us to reach out for calorie-laden, fast food. Our brain wants to get as much fuel onboard as quickly as possible. It doesn't stop to consider whether the fuel is long-lasting nor the fact it will cause us to crash an hour later when our sugar levels drop. We are on Autopilot.

Then during the afternoon because we hit another 'slump',

we don't want to move our body. We skip the gym and grab a caffeine-fuelled drink to give us a little 'pep' instead. We power on through the mountain of work. Then when we eventually get home, we nuke a microwave meal and numb ourselves with a box set or scroll through mindlessly on social media. We unwind by cracking open a bottle of wine.

Once all numbing activities have ceased, inconveniently that 'pep' we had earlier causes us to stare at the ceiling when it's time for a bit of shut-eye, (it takes up to 5 hours for half the caffeine to leave our system). Eventually, we drift off. Then as our body starts to get rid of the alcohol, we experience 'rebound alertness' and we are awake again. Rude. And so, the downward spiral continues.

We need our Captains to intervene. To take charge. To take the long view. To steer our Ship towards things that will enhance our energy and health.

I'm no angel 100% of the time. I like to do this stuff too. Recently, a client bought me a box of chocolates. I mindlessly ate half of them. My hand was on Autopilot, competently plucking the chocolates out of the box without consciously savouring each one as they entered my mouth. Next thing I know, I'm cross-eyed looking at my screen and at risk of headbutting it because I'm beginning to nod.

The next day, there were consequences. I'd screwed up, so I had to suck it up. I was knackered, the excess sugar had caused inflammation. My eyes had puffed up and looked like pee holes in the snow. I had brain fog and couldn't think clearly. My performance at work was affected. I wasn't as sharp as I could be. Everything took twice as long.

Research suggests that when people eat and drink less sugar, inflammatory markers in their blood decrease.[65]

The difference now is that I've educated myself and understand why I feel rubbish when I do, but I also know how to make corrections. In this chapter, I intend to stimulate your curiosity and begin signposting you towards things that you could look into further and potentially change.

ACTION:

Reflecting on your energy bank:

- What good energy deposits do you make?
- What bad energy withdrawals do you make?

The Root of All Evil - Inflammation

Traditionally we think of inflammation as being the swelling you get when you sprain your ankle or have swollen glands. Your body is reacting in the right way by getting your immune system to respond to tissue damage and fight infection. This is how inflammation should work.

However, in our modern society, we are unnecessarily triggering inflammation through, for example, cigarette smoke, air pollutants, chemicals in our water, processed foods and stress.[66] Your body responds to these unnatural chemicals and threatening situations by sending out danger signals which create inflammation to fight off the threat.

Now you might be thinking, so what? Inflammation is now recognised as a significant cause or complicating factor in diabetes, obesity, cancer, depression, heart disease[67] Inflammation also a contributing factor in Alzheimer's[68] and autoimmune diseases. It's the root of a lot of evils when it comes to health. Early signs of inflammation can include:

- Chronic fatigue (aka ME).
- Eczema, psoriasis or red and itchy skin.
- Puffy face or eye bags.
- Digestive problems e.g. bloating, constipation, diarrhoea, gas, nausea or vomiting.
- Aches and pains.

- Food intolerances.
- Headaches or migraines.
- Depression, anxiety or brain fog.

Our shine is dulled when we get inflammatory symptoms.

Recently I started hobbling around the house like I needed a hip-op. My husband said, 'What's up with you?' Sheepishly, I said, 'I shouldn't have drunk that rosé last night.' You might be thinking that's a big leap from wine to hobbling, but the truth is I know I can't tolerate rosé, beer, or copious amounts of white wine. My temple does however like the red type – thank the lord!

I know this because I have had a variety of food allergy tests carried out.[69] I have also visited a Kinesiologist who put test tubes of food on my stomach and waved my arm up and down. My body told her what I could and couldn't tolerate. It was like witchcraft – but in a good way. She also confirmed the unwanted news that I needed to avoid certain types of wine. Sounds like mumbo jumbo and hopefully, you've picked up that I am a real sceptic in the beginning, but if something works, I open my mind to it.

My symptoms continued through Christmas. We were away in Devon with my stepson and daughter-in-law and I had no pain during the day whilst out on our beach walks. I was absolutely fine. Nada. Nothing. It was only at night whenever I got up off the sofa.

At first, I thought perhaps the sofas in the rented cottage were at the wrong height and were exacerbating the rosé induced pain. I convinced myself it was the sofa's fault. (Chuckling as I type this). I felt quite embarrassed in front of my family; like I was attention-seeking!

Then I noticed that getting off the sofa was usually combined with getting a tasty inflammation-causing snack from the pantry or re-filling my glass with booze. My Captain was on holiday! I was ignoring the information coming through on my Bridge. It was Christmas!

Anyway, when we got home and eventually ate and drank our way through our pile of Christmas goodies, my symptoms stopped. I'd overloaded my system; created lots of inflammation and pain in the process.

Once I began fixing myself, I noticed that my daughter was suffering from severe heartburn to the extent where I'd been asked to collect her from school three times because they thought she'd been sick. Nope, poor thing had reflux and was getting crippling stomach ache having eaten certain foods. I know school dinners are supposed to be better, but pasta, pizza, bread rolls and cake all in one meal?

I repeated both food allergy testing processes with her, and there were themes. She can't tolerate sugar and wheat products which have raising agent in them. Long story short we eliminated the foods and her symptoms disappeared, as did my aches, pains, migraines, bloating and brain fog. My energy came back!

Having read a whole host of brilliant books, research papers and blogs, I now treat any pain or symptom as a sign that something isn't right. How often do we ignore these signals from our body and use medication as a sticking plaster? Got a migraine, right I'll load myself up with pills, make myself like a zombie as opposed to getting to the root cause, (it turned out to be stress combined with wheat).

Severe reflux? Right, pop antacids. If that doesn't work, get referred by a doctor for a hiatus hernia operation. That'll do it.

There have been so many 'symptoms' I've been able to resolve myself, naturally. But I needed the information from the tests to inform my Bridge, who incidentally now monitors any signals coming in relating to my health. My Captain then decides what to do about it. Woken up with spots? Is it stress or one milky cappuccino too many? Eliminate. Get back on track.

ACTION:

- Which foods / drinks do you suspect disagree with you?
- What physical symptoms do you get?
- What could you do about this?

So, I'm going to focus on food, as this is a major factor in inflammation, and you can be Captain of what you put in your mouth, whereas you have less influence over for example environmental factors. Food can also help you to make healthy deposits into your energy bank too, but first, let's look at how your body makes energy.

Your Duracell Batteries – Mitochondria

Food is the fuel for your body. The mitochondria are the converters; they transform the food we eat and the oxygen we breathe into useable energy. Mitochondria are known as the 'powerhouse of the cell'. Mitochondria are present in every cell of our body but are more concentrated in our muscles. They contain several enzymes and proteins that help process carbohydrates and fats obtained from the food we eat to release energy.

Our mitochondrial health influences how:

- Much energy we have.
- Quickly we age.
- Well we can focus.
- We fight off age-related diseases such as cancer, Alzheimer's and heart disease.

In Ben Angel's book *Unstoppable,* he explains that we can 'experience cognitive impairment, fatigue and brain fog' if the mitochondria in your brain, don't have a good energy supply.[70] Again if you're a knowledge worker, we don't exactly shine if we can't think clearly. Our mitochondria are damaged by:

- Toxins in our environment such as pollution and cleaning products.
- Certain medications and antibiotic use.
- Infections and allergens.
- Not effectively dealing with emotional trauma and stress (hence the previous chapters).
- A sedentary lifestyle (hence 'move your body' coming up).
- Processed foods or food sensitivities. You can get tested for food intolerances at your local chemist or there are companies on-line which will send you a kit in the post.

You can find a series of useful links to products and services I recommend on my resource page: https://www.beee.company/resources

To effectively charge our batteries to increase our energy and focus, stave off health issues and slow down the ageing process, we need to put good fuel in.

Donuts Make You Cross - Putting Good Fuel In

'Donuts Make You Cross' was the headline that first got me interested in how food affects our health and state of mind, having ignored the advice of my qualified nutritionist for ME recovery. What can I say; I am a stubborn mule. Sometimes I have to discover things for myself, as opposed to being told what to do.

So, if food is so important for our energy production and overall health, what should we be eating?

MitoQ, an organisation with expertise in mitochondria health recommends the following:

- Vegetables (excluding potatoes) are the best source of fibre, vitamins and minerals and should constitute most of your diet

- Protein should be sourced mainly from fish, poultry, beans and nuts and small amounts of red meat
- Whole-grain cereals should be chosen over refined grains such as white rice and flour
- Choose fruits at the peak of their freshness for the greatest nutritional value
- Use healthy oils when cooking or for salads, such as olive or coconut oils
- Steer clear of sugary drinks and fruit juices as they contain high amounts of fructose[71]

Back to doughnuts potentially making you cross. It turns out they can. In a study conducted by the University of California San Diego School of Medicine, they were able to demonstrate that the more dietary trans fatty acids, (dTFAs) we consume, the angrier we become. 'The study of nearly 1,000 men and women provides the first evidence linking dTFAs with adverse behaviours that impacted others, ranging from impatience to overt aggression. Adverse health effects of dTFAs have been identified in lipid levels, metabolic function, insulin resistance, oxidation, inflammation, and cardiac health.'[72]

If we're angry we not shining.

Here comes the food police warning. Examples of products containing dTFA's, and the products we should avoid include:

- Donuts, cakes, pies, cookies, biscuits, chocolate, margarine, crackers, microwave popcorn, fried fast food, frozen pizza, refined carbohydrates.

ACTION:
- To give your mitochondria a boost and avoid negatively impacting your state of mind what changes are you going to make to the food that you consume?

A final word about food. Dr. Michael Mosley is a British TV presenter, journalist and scientist has written a brilliant book called *The Clever Guts Diet: How to Revolutionise Your Body from the Inside Out* and looks at how we can positively influence our gut health. He provides more evidence as to the importance of the food we eat, 'We now know that the microbiome can influence everything from your immune system to your mood, from the allergies you develop to the amount of weight you put on. As you get older having lots of "good" bacteria living in your gut is increasingly important, as they will help you fight infection and prevent the onset of type 2 diabetes, as well as depression and common gut disorders.' You can find loads of useful information on his website.[73]

So, if we want to shine on the outside, we must take care of what we put inside so that we don't adversely affect our long-term health, state of mind and have more energy. Avoid the list of tasty stuff above…or slip it in now and then in small quantities (your taste buds and gut bacteria will eventually crave healthy things instead) and eat whole natural, unprocessed foodstuff that hasn't been tinkered with. Use the same care and attention with yourself, as you would with a growing child.

Self-Care: Treat Yourself Like a Baby

Parents learn a form of state management, doing everything they can to optimise the child's performance – code for preventing them from kicking off and making their lives difficult. Undoubtedly, parents and carers also want them to be happy and healthy too and give them the best chance of survival. So, why do we lose sight of this as adults? Why don't we look after ourselves in the same caring way? The short answer is, we think we can get away with it.

When babies are small, parents can spend a lot of time working out their rhythm. When their eating, sleeping, nappy changing and playtimes are. Mums, dads and carers can be seen dashing back home as the child's bedtime approaches, knowing that all hell will let loose the following day if they miss the allocated slot for sleep, or worse still the child gets over-tired, which results in a 4-hour bedtime routine.

There was a moment when I realised my daughter had hit terrible twos. Up until this stage she had been a very easy contented child and terrible twos was a suburban myth that more experienced parents told you about, to put you off child-rearing.

I was stood in the kitchen chatting to my child-free friend when suddenly, my daughter started doing a version of the 80s breakdance move, the caterpillar on the floor. My friend looked at my daughter and then at me and raised one of her beautifully shaped and pencilled eyebrows (because she had time) and asked me what she was doing. I sheepishly said, 'I don't know.' Then I realised that shock, horror the kitchen clock has stopped. She should have been bathed, had a story read to her and in bed by then.

If we are going to nurture ourselves like a baby it is important that in addition to eating nutritional food, we sleep, move our body and take appropriate self-care – otherwise, we are the ones having the tantrum! These are the final topics of this book.

Sleep

Most people love a good night's sleep, but why is it important? In a recent study, they identified that 'Sleep restriction selectively impairs sustained attention, executive function, and long-term memory.'[74] We're not going to shine if we're sleep deprived then! There are also lots of health benefits of getting plenty of zzz's too, including repair and detoxification. But how many hours do we need? The short answer is between 7-9 hours for your average healthy adult. Just as small children need a bedtime routine, so do adults and it is one of the first things I explore with clients when they mention they have sleep problems.

Having a bedtime routine helps signal to our body and mind that it will soon be time for sleep.

ACTION:

- What's your bedtime routine?

I first experienced not being able to sleep when I was 16. I used to work in a restaurant. If there was an award for the clumsiest waitress, I would win it. I used to walk into tables, drop puddings off the dessert trolley and smash glasses during speeches. But, the worst thing about the job was the fact that you had to remember the food orders, which was fine if you'd got a table of two and they only wanted starters – ideally the same thing.

When faced with a table of 20, it was a nightmare. I'd retain so much and then catch myself running to the serving hatch and blurting the order out at the grumpy chef. Then, of course, there was the risk of us both getting it wrong and you did not want to be around if the chef cocked up an order, which of course happened quite a lot when I was on shift.

I'd work until midnight, then get straight into bed once I got home. I couldn't understand why, having worked late (I was at college during the day too), and feeling so knackered that I couldn't drift off to sleep. There were two issues:

1. **I had no bedtime routine** and was expecting my brain to switch from beta brainwave (focussed concentration and alertness) to alpha brainwave, (relaxation and pre-sleep). I didn't have any bedtime habits which helped me to unwind after work and trigger alpha brainwaves. It's the equivalent of trying to shift from 6th gear to 1st – it doesn't work.

2. **My mind had been so busy** dealing with lots of information (some of it useless) both at college and then

at the restaurant, I hadn't allowed myself to go off-line and relax during the day to process this information. I kept myself focussed throughout the day (and in beta brainwave), which had a knock-on effect on my alpha brainwaves, which we need to experience before sleep. When our alpha activity is disrupted during the day, i.e. we haven't relaxed, it can make it difficult to relax when it is time for bed and impacts on the quality of our sleep.

Brainwaves

The lack of alpha brainwaves may also explain why I struggled to remember the food orders. In a study, they identified that people who were good at memory tasks with people who weren't so good at them. Those who excelled in the memory tasks had 1.25 Hz higher alpha frequencies.[75] So in other words, if we don't experience enough alpha brain waves, our memory is negatively affected. The bottom line is that if we spend too much time in beta (working / concentrating) with insufficient time in alpha (relaxation / switch off time) during the day, we get sleep and health problems. We need time in alpha to recover from beta. If you're an over-worker as I was, this is useful to know.

Now, the great news is, that going into alpha brain wave, is a naturally occurring process – we have to use our Bridge to notice that it's occurring, and get our Captain to take charge and ensure that you take advantage of this 'lull' in concentration.

Nathaniel Kleitman, an American physiologist and sleep researcher discovered the ultradian rhythm. The ultradian rhythm is responsible for our basic rest-activity cycle (BRAC). Every 90 minutes our body needs to rest; you may experience this as a light daydream or trance. When this occurs, there are several things you could do to switch off for a while during the day, (as opposed to powering through and keeping yourself in beta / focussed concentration):

- **Make a drink**. Note that if you have a caffeinated drink this will stimulate beta brainwaves again.
- **Go and stroke a furry friend.** You can increase levels of the stress-reducing hormone oxytocin and decrease the production of the stress hormone cortisol by stroking a pet.
- **Sit still and look out of the window** for a few minutes... watch the trees sway in the wind – allow yourself to daydream.
- **Take a proper lunch break!** Never mind, sitting at your desk and shovelling food in your mouth whilst still staring at your screen. It's a dirty place to eat anyway.
- **Listen to some music.** In a recent US study, the 'world's most relaxing song' called 'Weightless' by British band Marconi Union, was found that it could be as beneficial for calming a patient's nerves, as medication before surgery.[76]
- **Practice meditative breathing**, (coming up next). Closing your eyes encourages alpha brain waves.

ACTION:
- What changes are you going to make so that you encourage alpha brainwave activity during the day?

Meditative Breathing
As part of my daughter's bedtime routine which includes a bath and story, we also do some meditative breathing with her. Not only does this help her to relax into bedtime, but it also helps us to calm down too at the end of the day. We use 7/11 breathing for 2 minutes.

ACTION:
- Try this now for 2 minutes. If you have wearable technology such as a Fitbit which monitors your

heartbeat, notice what happens to your beats per minute before and after:

- Inhale through your nose for a count of 7 expanding your abdomen, (not your chest). It can help to put one hand on your stomach to focus your breath.
- Exhale through your mouth for a count of 11, contracting your abdomen.

There are countless studies on the benefits of meditation, and it is widely accepted as a treatment for anxiety and depression. Meditation can change your brain. A study found that the amygdala shrunk (the part of our brain responsible for fear and emotion) and the pre-frontal cortex (responsible for higher-order brain functions such as awareness, concentration and decision-making) became thicker.[77]

Preparing Ourselves for Sleep

So, having ensured we're getting enough relaxation during the day, the next step is to create the right environment for sleep. To prepare yourself for sleep:

- **Develop a bedtime routine** that involves activities which will encourage relaxation and a regular sleep and wake time... like a *bambino!*
- **Avoid screen time 30-60 minutes before sleep.**[78] The blue light which is emitted from our devices i.e. tablets, smartphones, computers and TV's affects how much of the sleep-related hormone melatonin we produce. When we make less melatonin, it can interrupt our sleep-wake cycle and make it more difficult to fall asleep.
- **Cut out anything too stimulating.** I can't watch a horror or read gory detective novels before I sleep. Stop working at least 1 hour before bed and no sneaking a peek at your

mail before you turn the lights out!

- **Stop drinking caffeine** *at least* 6 hours before your bedtime. A study reported that 'caffeine taken 6 hours before bedtime has important disruptive effects on sleep'.[79] This is even after we can no longer feel the buzz of the caffeine.
- **Complete bathing and exercising** 2 hours before sleep – this is to do with allowing your body to cool sufficiently so that you can sleep.
- **Finish eating** 3 hours before bed because digesting food also increases body temperature.
- **Use journaling** and / or EFT to empty your mind.
- **Consider using meditation and yoga**. Meditation relaxes the mind; yoga relaxes the body. I love anything by Gaiam.[80] They sell specific bedtime yoga sequences which I use, or you can find them on YouTube
- **Use a Bella Bee.**[81] This is my cheat option if I realise that I've not relaxed during the day and need some help switching between beta and alpha brainwaves. You plug the device into your phone and wear it on your head. It helps you to produce the appropriate brainwaves, using various programmes for sleep, meditation, concentration, anti-anxiety and anti-stress.
- **Finally, make sure your bedroom encourages sleep** by ensuring:
  - It isn't too hot or cold.
  - It is pitch black and there are no sources of light... even the standby light on your TV.
  - Your mattress, mattress topper, pillows and bedding are comfortable. Sleep has a big impact on our physical and mental health. Therefore, isn't it worth investing a few extra £'s to get a better night's sleep?

You can find a series of useful links to products and services I recommend on my resource page: https://www.beee.company/resources

ACTION:

- What changes are you going to make to enhance your sleep?

Move Your Body

Whilst we mustn't exercise too close to our bedtime, it can positively impact on our sleep. In a study, participants showed a 54% improvement in the time taken to get to sleep, a 36% reduction in night time waking and a 37% increase in total sleep time.[82]

There are lots of other reasons we should be exercising too. Firstly, exercise makes you feel good. We produce beta-endorphins which are mood enhancers. Moving also helps us to break out of any negative physiology we may have been adopting and ease tension.

Secondly, if we don't move every 90 minutes our fight or flight system kicks in and our body becomes stressed.

Thirdly, if we don't move every 25 minutes our lymphatic system (the system responsible for clearing toxins from our body and helping us to fight infection) begins to slow down.

Fourthly, is this shocking headline, 'Sitting around all day is as bad for your health as smoking.'[83] Following a study by Cambridge University's Professor Ulf Ekelund he found that you were 60% more likely to die prematurely if you sat at your desk for 8 hours. However, simply getting up to make a coffee can help and going for a 20-minute brisk walk will reduce the risk of premature death by between 16-30%.[84]

In 1991 Xpansions had a hit with 'Move Your Body (Elevation)'. I used to be a raver. This involved dancing for hours on end to house music in dark clubs, where the sweat dripped off the ceiling. I lived for my weekends. When I was 19 and on holiday in Magaluf, we went to one of the many clubs on The Strip and I got offered a job as a podium dancer! Whilst I still adore dancing even now, then Miss Stiff Knickers was aware that the office job at home was beckoning.

I'm typing this breathlessly having danced in my office. My husband calls me the 'Gadget Queen'. I like gadgets and technology when they save you time, effort and brainpower – not having to remember to do the minutia. I have Alexas all over the house and I wear a Fitbit. Every hour if I've been sat on my backside too long, my Fitbit prompts me to move. I get Alexa to take me back to the 90s for 5 minutes and I move my body. It's like a mini aerobic class, only without the leotard and tights. I dance like nobody is watching.

I appreciate that you might not be able to work from home or have the luxury of a private office these days. When I was gainfully employed and shared an office, I started up a lunchtime yoga group. Alternatively, I would march into town and shop! When I worked for a car seat manufacturing company, we adopted the exercise regime our Japanese customers used in the morning to get everyone warmed up for their day. Let your mind run wild with creative ways in which you could move your body each day.

ACTION:
- How do you like to move your body? What do you love?
- What daily activity could you build into your work-life? Keep it simple. Often the simplest changes that you adopt daily can be the most powerful.

Staying on Course
Finally, I keep myself on course with exercise, sleep and monitoring my stress and energy levels through my Fitbit.[85] I love this wearable technology. I can monitor the quality of my sleep. It's always a sure sign that I've been pushing things

too hard if my resting heart rate crashes and I have a higher percentage of deep sleep. This is because my heart is a muscle. If it's fatigued it doesn't beat as fast and my body is needing more deep sleep to heal itself. I've already shared that my clients use it to monitor when they have been triggered emotionally by looking at how fast their heart is beating – I do the same. Sometimes when I'm training, it looks as though I am running a race. However, it has taken time using my Bridge to assimilate this information and work out from my Fitbit statistics and how they relate to my health.

Visit the Mess Deck Daily

Having a self-care routine is especially important for workaholics. We must visit the Mess Deck daily, otherwise, we get stressed and sick. The Mess Deck is the counterbalance to our busy lives.

I encourage my clients to *live life in the space in between* and have a go-to list of things they do to look after themselves. I talk to them about 'Taking a mini holiday each day', as opposed to waiting for a holiday to fully unwind. When I was growing up in the 70s my best friend's mum used to go for a bike ride every night. She had four kids. Escaping and making time for ourselves, makes us better people. We buff up our shine every day when we adopt a self-care regime.

My go-to self-care activities include:

- Sitting with the dogs on the sofa with a cup of herbal tea.
- Reading a story to my daughter followed by 2 minutes of meditative breathing.
- Having a candlelit dinner at home with my hubby and then blasting out the tunes…maybe even dancing a little.
- Going for a walk in the nearby woods.
- Getting lost in a book.
- Yoga.

- Being pampered at the spa with my friend.

Don't wait for your holiday to relax, take a mini holiday each day.

ACTION:
- What things could you do each day to relax, recharge and look after yourself?
- What could you incorporate in your self-care routine?

Summary of Key Points
- Don't miss life by over-working. If we only live once, make it a brilliant once.
- Buff up your shine by ensuring that you charge your batteries and have all the energy you need to be brilliant; to shine.
- Do this by putting good fuel in, remembering that certain foods can damage your state of mind as well as your health.
- Prevent unnecessary inflammation, which is at the root of many diseases, by reducing stress, and eating unprocessed food.
- Practice great sleep habits. How well we sleep influences our state, energy, what we eat and how much we move the following day.
- Moving your body makes you feel good, live longer and aids sleep.
- Treat yourself like a baby; adopt a good self-care routine. Take a mini holiday each day.

Conclusion

I went for coffee with a friend this morning because I was on the home straight with this book. She was telling me about how another child had been cruel to her daughter. She reflected on how the children used to be in her daughter's class when she first joined in reception. So innocent. So pure. Without Baggage.

The girl that had been bullying her daughter was such a sweet little thing; full of joy, bounce and general excitement about life. As she matured these states have slowly dissipated. She's developed an attitude with her friends and teachers and has become surly. Her whole demeanour has changed. Her mouth is downturned. She glares at people in the playground as opposed to the old cheeky greeting, calling my friend by her first name, (we didn't do that in the 80s).

When my friend addressed the matter with the school, the young girl who'd been causing trouble, said 'I'm sorry, I've got a lot going on at home.' She's 10. The poor kid had been kicked out by her mother and was now being looked after by another relative.

I am not excusing her behaviour, I am empathising and wondering how hard it must be for that child. She must feel rejected by both parents.

Even before she was rejected by them, she was the child that was never allowed to attend her friends' parties, because her mum couldn't be bothered to drop her off, or turned up intoxicated on the one occasion when she was allowed to attend.

She was always the one who stood out for the wrong reasons in the school photo, always wearing the wrong colour uniform.

She was the one who played the piano beautifully in assembly but didn't have any relatives to appreciate her performance.

It sounds as though the kid has had it tough. My heart goes out to her. She's had a lot to deal with and is not shining on the outside, because she probably feels rotten on the inside.

This child will grow up into the type of adult that I will eventually end up working with. Never feeling good enough. Not feeling worthy of basic care and attention. Constantly having to prove that she is enough; the way she was made. Constantly proving through work and her relationships in life. Overextending herself, which eventually steals the joy out of work-life.

There are varying extremes of bad stuff that bend people out of shape and stop them from being the best version of themselves. Old stuff creating drag on their Ship, preventing them from shining in their work-life, directing them towards Destination Grim, as opposed to Destination Joy.

I hope that by now you have your personal blueprint for fixing the things that dull your shine and know how to steer yourself back to Destination Joy. Here's a reminder of the antidotes to imposter syndrome, workaholism, and stress:

Antidote #1: Know Your Co-ordinates

• Failing to recognise where you are currently:
    ○ Stuck in Groundhog Day on the screw up and repeat cycle.
    ○ Overworking to counter your imposter syndrome thoughts. Review your Workaholism Questionnaire from Chapter 1. What's different? What do you still need to change?
    ○ At risk of stress and burnout if nothing changes.
    ○ That *you* are responsible for your current situation...
• ...this is great news because *you* can fix this. The first step is to acknowledge your behaviour and thinking traps, otherwise, how do you know what needs to change? Then compassionately accept where you are at.

Antidote #2: Captain Your Ship

- You are the Captain of your Ship. Where are you going to *choose* to steer it to? Destination Grim or Destination Joy? Only *you* can make this change happen.

- You can point the finger of blame elsewhere for your current circumstances through victim or persecutor behaviour and hope that something will change. Or you can be the Brave Captain and take charge of your Ship.

- Captaining your Ship involves coming off Autopilot, which is your unconscious mind. At best we are 5% consciously in charge of our actions. For the less self-aware, this is 1% and where the opportunity lies.

- Every Captain must own and value their unique Treasure Trove of gifts, talents, and achievements. This helps keep imposter syndrome thoughts at bay.

- To Captain your Ship, you have to invest in *project me time*.

Antidote #3: Understand What Causes You to Sink

- Everyone has *some* baggage. However, carrying excess Baggage creates drag on your Ship making you doubt yourself and work harder, resulting in stress and ineffectiveness. Is it any wonder that you feel as though you are sinking?

- Your Baggage was created by childhood events, which trigger limiting beliefs, behaviours and emotions in adulthood. This impacts on the results and relationships in your work-life and can dull your shine.

- Raising awareness of what excess baggage you have on board, puts you back in charge as the Captain of your Ship so that you can offload it in Chapter 6.

- Taking a warts and all Snapshot of how things are right now will give you clues as to what you are going to work on during *project me time*. Review your Snapshot from Chapter 3 to see what has changed.

Antidote #4: Align Towards Your Stars

- When we align towards our purpose, strengths and values we increase our opportunity to shine and move closer to Destination Joy.

- Equally, when we are misaligned, we can feel like a failure, stressed, anxious, miserable, and as though we don't belong. This amplifies imposter syndrome thoughts; we are at Destination Grim.

- Overdoing a strength or value can become a weakness. Bring over-done strengths and values back into balance.

- Get clear on and *own* your strengths, gifts, talents, values and purpose. Then make changes to re-align towards them.

Antidote #5: Navigate to Destination Joy

- You can hope that work-life will magically sort itself out, but you run the risk of ending up at Destination Grim.

- The easiest option is maintaining the status quo, allowing yourself to get bored with work-life. Or you can excite yourself with brave plans which take you to Destination Joy. The choice is yours.

- Get clear on what Destination Joy is *for you*. What will work-life be like once you've dissipated your imposter syndrome and workaholism patterns?

- Destination Joy is represented by your Vision, Goals and Tasks. Create a plan. Go and review your plan from Chapter 5 now. How are you doing? Where have you got off course? What adjustments do you need to make? What successes have you had? Own them.

- Finally, stop dreaming, fantasising and visualising your desired outcome. This will reduce motivation because your brain thinks you've already attained it. Positively programme your mind by visualising all the small steps in between.

Antidote #6: Offload Excess Baggage

- Find out whether you are exceeding your baggage allowance by establishing your Adverse Childhood Experiences score. The higher your score, the higher your risk of health conditions.

- No fear though. This is the chapter where the magic starts to happen! You can offload your excess Baggage using Havening. It's like having a magic eraser. Haven any adult trigger by finding the root cause memory in your childhood.

- Havening allows you to reveal the best version of you! It's almost like cheating, as once the trigger has gone, your emotions, behaviour and results can change for the better.

- The more baggage you offload by 'erasing' the events which caused your imposter thoughts and over-working, the more buoyant, resilient, and effective you can become.

Antidote #7: Run a Tight Ship

- Once you have offloaded your excess baggage, it's important to *run a tight ship*. Not all limiting patterns of behaviour are down to nurture events in your childhood. When you fail to run a tight Ship you:

    o Say yes to tasks regardless of the impact on you personally.

    o Don't manage your time and people boundaries, which results in you always being 'switched on'. This leaves you with very little recuperation and fun time!

    o Give off the wrong vibes which makes it easier to be taken advantage of, resulting in you having too much to do.

- Therefore, you must:

    o Stop accepting unnecessary to do's that aren't yours. Be more like Bob, who would never take a job that wasn't his.

    o Ease up on taking responsibility for everyone and everything. Stop filling the gaps.

    o Create some work time boundaries. Make up your own rules. Remember Parkinson's Law in Chapter 7.

    o Identify what behaviour is acceptable and unacceptable. These are your people boundaries. Be the Brave Captain and enforce your rules.

- Implementing these behavioural changes will re-brand what you are known for, reducing the risk of you being taken advantage of, having too much to do and over-working.

Antidote #8: Develop Your Inner Captain

- If you allow your inner critic to rule the roost it will undermine you, and reinforce your imposter syndrome tendencies.

- Develop an Inner Captain. Start to like, love and support yourself as opposed to destabilising or condemning yourself.

- Learn to reduce use-less thoughts and gain new perspectives on situations.

- Increase useful thoughts by:

    o   Changing your inner voice tone and language.

    o   Switching thoughts off.

    o   Identifying your Plan B.

    o   Processing thoughts through journaling.

    o   Learning to laugh at yourself.

    o   Re-seeing your life for what it really is.

    o   Positively programming your mind through affirmations.

Antidote #9: Learn to Handle Rough Seas

- Your state of mind is your way of being at any moment. When you are in a positive state of mind you shine. Your shine is dulled and performance at work is affected when you are in a negative state of mind.

- The good news is that states of mind come and go like a bad smell and there are things you can do to influence how you feel.

- However, if you fall into the victim / persecutor thinking trap and fail to recognise that *you are responsible* for how you feel and *choose* to respond to a situation, you can end up at Destination Grim again.

- It's OK to have feelings. It's what makes you human. Work-life can throw you rough seas. Knowing how to handle them can help you to be more resilient and bounce back quicker from challenging events.

- You can reduce the impact of limiting states of mind by calming the waters using EFT. This then creates more space for joy, remembering that it has competition!

- Finally, having fun isn't just for kids, it's for you too. Make a date with the things that make you happy.

Antidote #10: Access the Mess Deck

- You can apply all the other learnings in this book, but if you don't implement what's in Chapter 10, you are still at risk of not shining. You must access the Mess Deck to rest, recharge and refuel in the *right way,* every day.

- Your potential to experience the joy of work-life can be diminished by pain, illness or exhaustion, which causes you to miss life. You end up surviving and not thriving.

- As a workaholic, you will be used to powering on through and ignoring your body's signals; failing to get to the root cause. This can result in using medication, alcohol, over-exercising or food as a sticking plaster.

- Learning to tune into what your body is telling you and then investigate the cause and taking corrective action, puts you back in charge as the Captain.

- The strategies in the Mess Deck counter your workaholic habits. You are encouraged to take a mini-holiday each day and treat yourself as if you were a treasured infant, giving yourself the best possible chances to thrive and shine.

Don't get stuck in Groundhog Day. You can do it. Keep going… or get in touch with me ☺. I'd love to help: estelle@beee.company

And now my lovely, we have reached the end of our journey together. Being able to press the reset button and return a human being to the way they were made like that little girl was in reception; full of joy, bounce and general excitement about work-life. Their excess Baggage cleared. Their vigour for their vocation renewed. Their unhelpful behaviours, habits and beliefs pruned. Owning their spot on this planet. This is my aspiration for all my clients either through coaching, training or reading this book. I hope you too can beee…yourself. Be brilliant. Shine.

About Estelle Read

Estelle set up Beee in 2005 to help organisations and their people optimise productivity, performance, success and wellbeing so that they lead their best business-life. She does this by getting her clients to dream big; clear obstacles; refocus on what's important; develop talent and enhance effectiveness. Estelle works with a variety of clients including Toyota, JP Morgan, The Law Society, NHS, Police Mutual, Huub, Marston Group, Vetoquinol and NFU Mutual.

Having been in the Human Resources (HR) industry for almost 30 years, she understands work-based mental health issues and the impact this has on both employee and employer from a performance perspective. As a Chartered Fellow of the Chartered Institute of Personnel and Development, (CIPD), a qualified coach and practitioner in many therapeutic disciplines, she has coached and trained more than 10,000 people.

Work with Estelle Read

Would you like to work with Estelle? She offers psychometric testing, seminars, training programmes, team events, group and 1-2-1 coaching on a range of topics, either face to face or virtually including:

- Assertiveness
- Coaching and Mentoring
- Communication
- Confidence
- Emotional Intelligence
- Inner Brilliance, Outer Shine (IBOS) Programme
- Leadership
- Networking
- Neuro Linguistic Programming (NLP)
- Personal Effectiveness
- Presentation Skills
- Resilience
- Stress Management and Wellbeing
- Time Management
- Vision, Values and Strategic Planning

Alternatively, you could join her Inner Brilliance Outer Shine Facebook group of like-minded people and get access to free content. You can find details here: https://www.beee.company/resources

You can connect, subscribe, listen to podcasts or book a free discovery session (subject to availability) here:

- Link Tree: https://linktr.ee/EstelleAtBeee
- Email: estelle@beee.company
- Website: www.beee.company
- Social Media: @EstelleAtBeee

Endnotes

1. https://journals.plos.org/plosone/article?id=10.1371/journal.pone.0152978
2. https://www.sciencedaily.com/releases/2016/05/160525084547.htm
3. https://icd.who.int/browse11/l-m/en#/http://id.who.int/icd/entity/129180281
4. https://www.kronos.com/resources/employee-burnout-crisis
5. Perkins, A. (1994). Saving money by reducing stress. Harvard Business Review. 72(6):12.
6. https://www.sciencedaily.com/terms/sympathetic_nervous_system.htm
7. https://www.telegraph.co.uk/news/science/science-news/8316534/Welcome-to-the-information-age-174-newspapers-a-day.html
8. https://pubsonline.informs.org/doi/10.1287/mnsc.2014.2115
9. http://mpowir.org/wp-content/uploads/2010/02/Download-IP-in-High-Achieving-Women.pdf
10. *On Death and Dying: What the Dying Have to Teach Doctors, Nurses, Clergy and Their Own Families* (2014) by Elizabeth Kubler-Ross
11. *The Biology of Belief – Unleashing the Power of Consciousness, Matter & Miracles* by Bruce Lipton, (2005)
12. https://www.youtube.com/watch?v=eB-vh6VWdcM
13. https://www.youtube.com/watch?v=eB-vh6VWdcM
14. https://www.historyonthenet.com/the-titanic-why-did-the-titanic-sink
15. *Emotional Intelligence: Why it can Matter More Than IQ* by Daniel Goleman (1996)
16. https://elifesciences.org/articles/02798
17. https://www.brucelipton.com/blog/how-my-research-

linked-epigenetics

18. https://www.karpmandramatriangle.com/

19. https://psychology.wikia.org/wiki/Morris_Massey

20. http://img.strengths.institute/institute/docs/The%20 Clifton%20StrengthsFinder%202.0%20Technical%20 Report.pdf

21. https://link.springer.com/article/10.1007%2Fs10902-017-9864-z

22. *Authentic Happiness: Using the new Positive Psychology to Realize Your Potential for Lasting Fulfilment* by Martin E. P. Seligman, (2002).

23. *Now, Discover Your Strengths. How to Develop Your Talents and Those of the People you Manage* by Marcus Buckingham and Donald O. Clifton (2002).

24. https://www.gallupstrengthscenter.com/

25. http://www.viacharacter.org/

26. https://strengthsprofile.com/en-gb/buy

27. https://neuroscienceschool.com/2019/06/20/why-visualization-doesnt-work-to-make-your-dreams-a-reality/?mc_cid=a43c3e8779&mc_eid=a88b2855a4

28. *Built To Last: Successful Habits Of Visionary Companies, (Tenth Anniversary Edition),* by Jim Collins and Jerry Porras, (2005).

29. https://www.sciencedaily.com/releases/2019/10/191029140738.htm

30. https://www.psychologytoday.com/us/blog/the-athletes-way/201211/the-neurochemicals-happiness

31. http://energycut.com.au/business/wp-content/uploads/2015/02/Dominican-Research-Cited-In-Forbes-Article.pdf

32. http://news.mit.edu/2014/in-the-blink-of-an-eye-0116

33. *The Worst Is Over: What To Say When Every Moment Counts,* by Judith Acosta and Judith Prager, (2002).

34. https://www.ncbi.nlm.nih.gov/pubmed/9635069

35. http://www.hsj.gr/medicine/impact-of-a-singlesession-of-

havening.php?aid=7273&fbclid=IwAR1HTsZLPZoaLdpqv
od_FubGP4mVJAAbpSFSB-Rb_hkuRqpkgB_yViONaPU

36. https://havening.org/about-havening/disclaimer
37. https://havening.org/about-havening/overview
38. *Why You Get More Done When You Work Less* by Alex Pang, (2016).
39. https://news.gallup.com/businessjournal/23146/Too-Many-Interruptions-Work.aspx
40. https://www.psychologytoday.com/us/blog/words-can-change-your-brain/201208/why-word-is-so-dangerous-say-or-hear?utm_source=FacebookPost&utm_medium=FBPost&utm_campaign=FBPost
41. https://pubmed.ncbi.nlm.nih.gov/18257652/
42. *The Moral Animal: Why We Are, the Way We Are: The New Science of Evolutionary Psychology* Robert Wright, Vintage, (1995)
43. Positive affect and the complex dynamics of human flourishing. Fredrickson BL, Losada MF. Am Psychol. 2005 Oct;60(7):678-86
44. Happiness unpacked: positive emotions increase life satisfaction by building resilience. Cohn MA, Fredrickson BL, Brown SL, Mikels JA, Conway AM. Emotion. 2009 Jun;9(3):361-8
45. *Feel The Fear And Do It Anyway: How to Turn Your Fear and Indecision into Confidence and Action* by Susan Jeffers, (2001).
46. *How to be Brilliant. Change Your Ways in 90 Days!* by Michael Heppell, (2004)
47. *Lost Connections: Uncovering the Real Causes of Depression – and the Unexpected Solutions* by Johann Harri, (2018).
48. *Star Wars, The Empire Strikes Back*, (1980)
49. https://www.ncbi.nlm.nih.gov/pubmed/12585811
50. https://www.cambridge.org/core/journals/advances-in-psychiatric-treatment/article/emotional-and-physical-health-benefits-of-expressive-writing/

ED2976A61F5DE56B46F07A1CE9EA9F9F

51. https://www.scientificamerican.com/article/writing-can-help-injuries-heal-faster/

52. *Rich Habits: The Daily Success Habits of Wealthy Individuals* by Thomas C Corley, (2009).

53. https://link.springer.com/article/10.1007%2Fs00101-015-0001-2

54. https://positivepsychology.com/neuroscience-of-gratitude/#:~:text=It%20produces%20a%20feeling%20of%20long-lasting%20happiness%20and,our%20emotions%2C%20and%20they%20make%20us%20feel%20%E2%80%98good%E2%80%99

55. https://hbr.org/2014/12/how-your-state-of-mind-affects-your-performance

56. *Emotional Agility: Get Unstuck, Embrace Change and Thrive in Work and Life* by Susan David (2016).

57. https://www.the-emotions.com/robert-plutchik.html

58. Gottman, J. M., Katz, L. F., & Hooven, C. (1997). Meta-emotion: How families communicate emotionally. Hillsdale, NJ, England: Lawrence Erlbaum Associates, Inc.

59. https://greatergood.berkeley.edu/article/item/how_to_deal_with_feeling_bad_about_your_feelings

60. http://s3.amazonaws.com/eft-academic-articles/Clinical-EFT-as-an-Evidence-Based-Practice-for-the-Treatment-of-Psychological-and-Physiological-Conditions.pdf

61. https://articles.mercola.com/sites/articles/archive/2013/12/26/emotional-freedom-technique.aspx

62. https://link.springer.com/article/10.1007/s11482-009-9091-9

63. *Eat Move Sleep: How Small Choices Lead to Big Changes* by Tom Rath (2013)

64. https://www.ncbi.nlm.nih.gov/pubmed/19620907

65. https://www.ncbi.nlm.nih.gov/pubmed/24418247

66. https://theconversation.com/explainer-what-is-inflammation-and-how-does-it-cause-disease-84997

67. http://content.time.com/time/magazine/article/0,9171,993419,00.html

68. https://www.sciencedaily.com/releases/2012/07/120702134820.htm

69. https://www.testyourintolerance.com/

70. *Unstoppable: A 90 Day Plan to Biohack Your Mind and Body for Success* by Ben Angel (2018).

71. https://www.mitoq.com/blog/which-foods-help-your-mitochondria

72. https://www.sciencedaily.com/releases/2012/03/120313122504.htm

73. https://cleverguts.com/

74. https://www.sciencedirect.com/science/article/pii/S0149763417301641

75. https://link.springer.com/article/10.1007/BF01128991

76. https://www.independent.co.uk/arts-entertainment/music/news/relaxing-song-best-weightless-marconi-union-youtube-surgery-anxiety-a9011971.html

77. https://journals.plos.org/plosone/article?id=10.1371/journal.pone.0064574

78. https://www.livescience.com/53874-blue-light-sleep.html#:~:text=Research%20has%20found%20that%20exposure%20to%20blue%20light,is%20more%20sensitive%20to%20this%20type%20of%20light.

79. https://jcsm.aasm.org/doi/10.5664/jcsm.3170

80. https://www.gaiam.com/

81. https://www.bellabee.org/

82. https://www.sciencedaily.com/releases/2008/06/080611071129.htm

83. https://www.thesun.co.uk/news/1513960/sitting-around-all-day-is-as-bad-for-your-health-as-smoking/

84. https://www.cam.ac.uk/research/news/lack-of-exercise-responsible-for-twice-as-many-deaths-as-obesity

85. https://www.fitbit.com/uk/home

References and Further Reading

Bandler, R. and Grinder, J. (1979), *Frogs into Princes: Neuro Linguistic Programming*, Utah, Real People Press

Blair, L. (2013), *Birth Order: What Your Position In The Family Really Tells You About Your Character*, Great Britain, Piatkus

Buckingham, M. and Clifton, D. O. (2001), *Now Discover Your Strengths: How To Develop Your Talents And Those Of The People You Manage*, (2002), Great Britain, Simon & Schuster UK Ltd

Carson, R. (2003), *Taming Your Gremlin: A Surprisingly Simple Method For Getting Out Of Your Own Way (Revised Edition)*, United States of America, Harper Collins

Collins, J. and Porras, J. I. (2005) *Built To Last: Successful Habits Of Visionary Companies, (Tenth Anniversary Edition)*, London., Random House Business Books

Cope, A. and Oattes, G. (2018), *Shine: Rediscovering Your Energy, Happiness and Purpose*, United Kingdom, John Wiley & Sons Ltd

Craig, G. (2008), *The EFT Manual*, USA, Energy Psychology Press

David, S. (2017), *Emotional Agility: Get Unstuck, Embrace Change, and Thrive in Work and Life*, Great Britain, Penguin Life

Goleman, D. (1996), *Emotional Intelligence: Why It Can Matter More Than IQ*, Great Britain, Bloomsbury Publishing Plc

Heppell, M. (2004), *How To Be Brilliant: Change Your Life In 90 Days*, Harlow, Pearson Education Limited

James, T. and Woodsmall, W (1988), *Time Line Therapy And The Basis Of Personality*, Capitola, Meta Publications

Kotter, J. P. (1996) *Leading Change*, USA, Harvard Business School Press

Linley, A. and Bateman, T. (2018) *The Strengths Profile Book: Finding What You Can Do + Love To Do And Why It Matters*, Birmingham, Capp Press

Lipton, B. (2015), *The Biology of Belief: Unleashing the Power of*

Consciousness, Matter & Miracles, UK, Hay House

O'Connor, J. (2001) *NLP Workbook: A Practical Guide To Achieving The Results You Want*, London, Harper Collins

Silverthorn, M. S. and Overdurf, J. (2000), *Dreaming Realities: A Spiritual System To Create Inner Alignment Through Dreams*, UK, Crown House Publishing Ltd

Sinek, S. (2009), *Start With Why: How Great Leaders Inspire Everyone To Take Action*, London, Penguin Group

Stewart, I. and Joines, V. (2002), *TA Today: A New Introduction to Transactional Analysis*, UK, Lifespace Publishing

Syed, M. (2016), *Black Box Thinking: Marginal Gains And The Secrets of High Performance*, Great Britain, John Murray (Publishers) An Hachette UK Company

Peters, S. (2011), *The Chimp Paradox: The Mind Management Programme for Confidence, Success and Happiness*, UK, Vermillion

Ruden, R. A. (2011), *When The Past Is Always Present: Emotional Traumatization, Causes and Cures,* USA, Routledge

BUSINESS
BOOKS

Business Books

Business Books publishes practical guides
and insightful non-fiction for beginners and professionals.
Covering aspects from management skills, leadership and
organizational change to positive work environments, career
coaching and self-care for managers, our books are a valuable
addition to those working in the world of business.

15 Ways to Own Your Future
Take Control of Your Destiny in Business and in Life
Michael Khouri
A 15-point blueprint for creating better collaboration, enjoyment, and success in business and in life.
Paperback: 978-1-78535-300-0 ebook: 978-1-78535-301-7

The Common Excuses of the Comfortable Compromiser
Understanding Why People Oppose Your Great Idea
Matt Crossman
Comfortable compromisers block the way of anyone trying to change anything. This is your guide to their common excuses.
Paperback: 978-1-78099-595-3 ebook: 978-1-78099-596-0

The Failing Logic of Money
Duane Mullin
Money is wasteful and cruel, causes war, crime and dysfunctional feudalism. Humankind needs happiness, peace and abundance. So banish money and use technology and knowledge to rid the world of war, crime and poverty.
Paperback: 978-1-84694-259-4 ebook: 978-1-84694-888-6

Mastering the Mommy Track
Juggling Career and Kids in Uncertain Times
Erin Flynn Jay
Mastering the Mommy Track tells the stories of everyday working mothers, the challenges they have faced, and lessons learned.
Paperback: 978-1-78099-123-8 ebook: 978-1-78099-124-5

Modern Day Selling
Unlocking Your Hidden Potential
Brian Barfield
Learn how to reconnect sales associates with customers and unlock hidden sales potential.
Paperback: 978-1-78099-457-4 ebook: 978-1-78099-458-1

The Most Creative, Escape the Ordinary, Excel at Public Speaking Book Ever
All The Help You Will Ever Need in Giving a Speech
Philip Theibert
The 'everything you need to give an outstanding speech' book, complete with original material written by a professional speech-writer.
Paperback: 978-1-78099-672-1 ebook: 978-1-78099-673-8

On Business And For Pleasure
A Self-Study Workbook for Advanced Business English
Michael Berman
This workbook includes enjoyable challenges and has been de-signed to help students with the English they need for work.
Paperback: 978-1-84694-304-1

Small Change, Big Deal
Money as if People Mattered
Jennifer Kavanagh
Money is about relationships: between individuals and between communities. Small is still beautiful, as peer lending model, micro-credit, shows.
Paperback: 978-1-78099-313-3 ebook: 978-1-78099-314-0

Readers of ebooks can buy or view any of these bestsellers by clicking on the live link in the title. Most titles are published in paperback and as an ebook. Paperbacks are available in traditional bookshops. Both print and ebook formats areavailable online.

Find more titles and sign up to our readers' newsletter at

http://www.jhpbusiness-books.com/

Facebook: https://www.facebook.com/JHPNonFiction/

Twitter: @JHPNonFiction